Pets have souls too

By the same author

Ripples (Capall Bann, 2001)

Come Back to Life (Capall Bann, 2005)

Past Life Angels (O Books, 2005)

Souls Don't Lie (O Books, 2006)

The Tree That Talked (O Books, 2007)

Night of the Unicorn (O Books, 2008)

How to Be Happy (O Books, 2008)

Past Life Meditation CD (Meditation Music, 2004)

Pets have souls too

JENNY SMEDLEY

HAY HOUSE

Australia • Canada • Hong Kong • India
South Africa • United Kingdom • United States

First published and distributed in the United Kingdom by:
Hay House UK Ltd, 292B Kensal Rd, London W10 5BE. Tel.: (44) 20 8962 1230; Fax:
(44) 20 8962 1239. www.hayhouse.co.uk

Published and distributed in the United States of America by:
Hay House, Inc., PO Box 5100, Carlsbad, CA 92018-5100. Tel.: (1) 760 431 7695 or
(800) 654 5126; Fax: (1) 760 431 6948 or (800) 650 5115. www.hayhouse.com

Published and distributed in Australia by:
Hay House Australia Ltd, 18/36 Ralph St, Alexandria NSW 2015. Tel.: (61) 2 9669
4299; Fax: (61) 2 9669 4144. www.hayhouse.com.au

Published and distributed in the Republic of South Africa by:
Hay House SA (Pty), Ltd, PO Box 990, Witkoppen 2068. Tel./Fax: (27) 11 467 8904.
www.hayhouse.co.za

Published and distributed in India by:
Hay House Publishers India, Muskaan Complex, Plot No.3, B-2, Vasant Kunj, New Delhi
– 110 070. Tel.: (91) 11 4176 1620; Fax: (91) 11 4176 1630. www.hayhouse.co.in

Distributed in Canada by:
Raincoast, 9050 Shaughnessy St, Vancouver, BC V6P 6E5. Tel.: (1) 604 323 7100; Fax:
(1) 604 323 2600

A catalogue record for this book is available from the British Library.

ISBN 978-1-84850-090-7

Printed and bound in Great Britain by CPI Bookmarque, Croydon CR0 4TD.

I dedicate this book to all the animals who have been prepared to share their consciousness with me.

I wouldn't be here today, doing what I'm doing, if it weren't for my soulmate of many lifetimes, Tony, so this book is also dedicated to him.

I'd also like to thank all the wonderful people who've co-operated with me during the writing of this book, and answered my interminable questions about their stories. They've shown great patience and fortitude during their interviews, by having to relive very emotional moments in their lives.

I'd also like to thank Hay House for this opportunity.

Rainbow Bridge

Just this side of heaven is a place called Rainbow Bridge. When an animal dies that has been especially close to someone here, that pet goes to the Rainbow Bridge. There are meadows and hills for all of our special friends so they can run and play together. There is plenty of food, water and sunshine, and our friends are warm and comfortable. All the animals that had been ill and old are restored to health and vigour; those who were hurt or maimed are made whole and strong again, just as we remember them in our dreams of days and times gone by. The animals are happy and content, except for one small thing: they miss someone very special, someone who was left behind.They all run and play together, but the day comes when suddenly one stops and looks into the distance. His bright eyes are intent; his eager body begins to quiver. Suddenly he breaks from the group, flying over the green grass, faster and faster.

You have been spotted, and when you and your special friend finally meet, you cling together in joyous reunion, never to be parted again. The happy kisses rain upon your face; your hands again caress the beloved head, and you look once more into those trusting eyes, so long gone from your life, but never absent from your heart. Then you cross the Rainbow Bridge together.

Author Unknown

Contents

Introduction

Animals were always my first love. Their purity of spirit and their constant ability to love unconditionally often made me wish for a world totally populated with just animals, when I was young. Animals didn't judge me and animals responded to me with openness and honesty. It didn't matter to me whether an animal was cute and furry in a conventional way, spiky and prickly like a hedgehog, or derided and hated, like a rat or mouse. I loved them all the same. I had a strong empathy with them right from the time I could walk and speak.

My very earliest memory of my first connection to an animal is a little fuzzy, because it took place when I was only two years old, but when I was older my mum filled in the gaps.

Sally

Although my family weren't really all that fussed about having animals in the house, they'd been persuaded to take on a two-year-old dog called Sally. Sally was a bull terrier cross boxer. She was very striking to look at, being smooth haired, mostly black with just a white bib, and ginger accessories like her eyebrows, bracelets on her legs and a thin ginger line dividing her white bib from the rest of her black coat. Mum had been assured she was a well-behaved, non-aggressive dog, but she didn't suspect just how thoroughly I was going to test that guarantee out!

On the day of her arrival, Sally was given a big marrowbone and let into the garden with it, where she soon settled down and started chewing contentedly. A few minutes later Mum was distracted by the arrival of a neighbour, and when she came back into the kitchen and looked out of the window, she saw, to her horror, her two-year-old toddler (me) tottering across the grass to the dog and bending down to grab the bone from her jaws. Not having time to do anything more than yell out of the window, which might have triggered a bad reaction from the dog, my mother could only watch in fear at what might happen next. Apparently, after I'd nonchalantly reached down and grabbed the bone, I walked off with it, with poor Sally following along behind me. That was the start of a lifelong friendship.

Because Sally was two and I was two when she came to the family, we grew together. She was my constant escort and guardian. I remember my Uncle Phil, who was a very kindly soul, waving an arm around my head once as he tried to swat a fly away from me. Thinking he was going to hit me, Sally leapt between us and grabbed and held his arm. She didn't bite him, she never bit, but she held him tight all the same. From quite a young age I was completely safe to roam around the countryside, so long as I had my guardian, Sally, with me. She was my playmate and my best friend for 12 years, and we went everywhere together.

Feeding the Swans

When I was still quite small, I scared Mum some more with my apparently casual attitude to animals. We used to visit Southsea, in Hampshire, for holidays at my Aunt May's hotel. What I used to like best was feeding the seagulls as they soared overhead. I soon learned that if I threw the bread as high as I could, one of these supreme flying acrobats would snatch it out of the air before it could fall to Earth. I really admired their peerless ability in the air. One particular day Mum took me to the park and I happily wandered around while she sat on a bench. The next thing she knew, I was surrounded by about seven swans. Unbeknownst to Mum I'd had half a loaf in my pocket and had decided to offer it to these really big 'seagulls'. Mum said the swans were taller than me, and she really didn't know what to do as I stood in the centre of a circle of huge white birds, with their flashing beaks and flapping wings. As she rushed over, though, she realized to her amazement that I had the situation totally under control. I was giving each bird in turn a piece of bread, scolding any that tried to grab an extra crumb, pushing any greedy beaks aside, and the swans, amazingly, were being really gentle with me. When all the bread was gone I just told them all to go away, and they did.

Monkey Business

The next strong animal-connection-related event I can recall, apart from a constant life-long desire to have my own pony – ever since I'd been able to vocalize the need – and my love for various rabbits and other pets I had, was with my brother's monkey. My brother was the only other person in the family who showed a strong desire to own a pet, but only a monkey, so that might have been more to do with the kudos of having an exotic pet rather than loving animals in general. The monkey's name showed no originality at all: Cheetah, after the chimp by the same name in the Tarzan films. I don't know what type of monkey Cheetah was, as I was only about eight years old at the time, but he looked like a small chimpanzee. He had a large pen in the garden and was a little difficult to handle, often nipping people. Mum told me that one day she looked out of the window to see me walking round the garden, with Cheetah slung on my hip, his arms around me, much in the way a mother might carry a toddler. I can even remember the feeling of doing it, with the monkey's warm little body clamped to mine. I had no fear at all. Cheetah was re-homed to a zoo not long after that, where he was able to live with others of his kind, partly because I kept saying it should be so, and that he wasn't happy in his cage, and that was why he nipped people.

An Injured Bird

I became a real tomboy, and my memories are of endless, hazy, sunny days spent outdoors in the company of animals as much as possible. But my rapport with animals, and my compassion for them, soon became a bit of a burden to me, because the slightest hurt committed to any helpless creature, human or animal, was like a deep hurt to me. I distinctly remember the day I realized I was different from the rest of my family. We were on the way to the shops in the car when we came upon a bird – it was a red-legged partridge – just sitting in the middle of the road, not even trying to run away from the approaching car, let alone fly. 'Stop the car!' I yelled. My dad did stop the car, but he wasn't best pleased. 'There's nothing you can do,' he told me, with a hint of impatience.

I got out of the car and approached the bird. It staggered as if drunk, and I cupped my hands around it and lifted it up. It had no marks or injuries on it, and its wings and legs were undamaged, but it had obviously been struck a glancing blow by a car, which had stunned it. I took it over to the side of the road, straddled the wire fence and carefully placed it in the undergrowth, where it could take its time to recover in safety. I was certain it would soon be back to normal.

To me this bird was everything to do with us, whereas to my family it was of no concern, and I was just being 'silly'. I puzzled over this for years. How could one person be totally unable to leave an injured creature to fend for itself, whereas other people could walk away without a thought? I almost fell out with various members of my family on many issues relating to what they did and what went on in their homes over the years – holes in fascia boards they would fill in to stop housemartins nesting inside sheds, bats that were crushed to death because they had invaded a bedroom by accident, a cat my dad left for dead after he'd hit it with his car, without checking if it was still alive or informing its owners, who might have spent months searching for their pet. I'd get furious – but don't get me wrong, my family aren't deliberately cruel or heartless people. They are good people, but they just didn't connect to animals at all, whereas I loved animals more than I loved most people.

Communicating

As I reached my teens, while other girls were obsessed with boyfriends and make-up, I was roaming around, usually dressed in jodhpurs, usually pretty grubby, and usually trying to rescue some animal or other. I was always bringing home waifs and strays and installing them in various boxes and cages while I tried to help them recover from whatever injuries had befallen them.

One pivotal time that I vividly recall, which made me understand why and how I had such a great connection to animals, was when a sparrow had flown into our glass back door and was lying on the ground, unable to move. I picked it up. The poor little thing's tail was cocked up at a very odd angle, like a wren's, and it was obviously in great distress. I held the bird gently in my hands, wondering what to do for the best. To my astonishment, I heard the words in my mind: *My tail, put my tail back.* Not really believing I could work a miracle, not sure if I'd really heard anything, and terrified of hurting the bird more, I nevertheless carefully manipulated the tail downwards, towards its correct position. Suddenly, with a satisfying 'click', the tail popped back into its socket and was straight again. With total joy I opened my hands and the bird flew off, straight and true. I was ecstatic, and suddenly had the revelation that my connection to animals wasn't just some mysterious sort of rapport, they were actually communicating with me. It was just that, up til then, I'd been too young to understand the concept.

After that this communication started to happen on a regular basis. When I'd find injured animals, they'd be able to tell me what they needed. Most of them wanted a quiet, dark, warm place to rest, sometimes to recover, and some of them just wanted a private place to die in peace.

Sometimes it was very hard to hear animals' pleas and not be able to help as much as I'd have liked. One time, after Tony and I were married, we were driving along the motorway when, perched right on the white line that divided the slow lane from the hard shoulder, there was a cat. It wasn't close to death, and it was sitting up, but it was obviously injured and unable to move, and equally obviously terrified. *Help me!* I heard in my mind. All this I saw and heard in a spilt second, as we flashed past. But by the time my mind had recognized what I'd seen and heard in that spilt second, we were already several hundred yards down the road, and the traffic was moving nose-to-tail and very fast. Stopping quickly wasn't an option. Anyway, stopping on the motorway, even on the hard shoulder, unless broken down, was very dangerous and certainly illegal. Even as I thought about what to do for the best we were travelling at speed ever further away. Then I saw a motorway phone ahead.

Tony pulled over, hazard lights flashing. I opened the little door of the emergency phone booth, pulled out the phone and dialled the number, conscious of the stream of traffic thundering by, much too close for comfort. This only made me even more aware of what that poor cat was going through, as it was much closer to the carriageway than I was. The man who answered the phone didn't seem to think an injured cat was much of an emergency. It was for the *cat*, I told him. In the end I had to tell him the animal was causing a hazard, that cars were swerving round it, and that there was bound to be a big accident, which would be his fault if he did nothing. He agreed to send out an emergency vehicle to pick up the cat. All day I reached out intuitively, hoping to hear more from the cat, but there was nothing. I thought perhaps it had died before it could be helped, or perhaps we were too far away by then for it to reach me. I gave up, but then on the way home we passed that spot again, and of course I looked across the carriageways and thought of the cat, picturing it in my mind. All of a sudden I could sense the flash of relief that the cat had felt as it had been picked up, so I knew it had been taken to help.

Empathy with Animals

The empathy I feel with animals has made life very difficult at times, and as I have grown and forged my own spiritual path, I still have daily problems coping with the feelings I get. Seeing people ill-treating a defenceless animal makes my blood boil. If I see a dog locked in a car on a hot day, I can't walk away, because the dog will call out to me to help it. Many times I've waited and confronted the owner when they've returned to their car, asking them to sit locked in it for a while themselves and see how they like it. Once or twice when they've been too long, I've phoned the police or RSPCA and had them break into the cars. One time the car wasn't locked and I was able to get a beautiful but very distressed Golden Retriever out, much to the surprise and anger of the owner when he returned from an outdoor bowls match. Luckily I was able to convince him that I'd done the right thing, and eventually he thanked me for saving his dog.

When I see a container full of sheep, pigs or cattle on their way to the abattoir, I can feel their distress and confusion. They often know exactly where they're going, having picked up images from their handlers, so I sense their fear as well. The only help I can offer in that moment is to envision wrapping that lorry-load in the light and warmth of their creator, and let them go with love. I'm sure that in a couple of hundred years man will look back on these times with the guilt he now feels over the way slaves were once kept and treated.

Sedona, Arizona

Despite the distress it can cause, it can be very useful to have a strong rapport with the animal kingdom, because if you're lucky you can access their wisdom and knowledge, and use their strong instincts where yours may have failed. Something that happened while Tony and I were visiting the stunning town of Sedona, in Arizona, proved this to me.

Sedona is an oasis of green in the middle of the hot, dusty Arizona countryside. It's surrounded by the most beautiful, wind-sculpted red rocks, all of which have names inspired by their shapes: Cathedral, Bell, Castle and Kachina Woman among them. There are also four powerful energy vortexes in the area, each one near a different red rock.

We wanted to get up close to Kachina Woman, which you can't see from the road as it's hidden by a knoll. It's quite difficult to walk to without a guide, as the trail is not at all clear. We set off from the nearest car park and soon became quite lost. The temperature was 100 degrees, and Arizona has rattlesnakes as well as scorpions, black widow spiders and tarantulas, among others, so we were a little nervous. Before long we realized that we'd been right to be nervous, because we were hopelessly lost.

Every bush and patch of sandy soil looked the same, and soon we had no idea where the rock was or, more worryingly, which way would lead us back to our car. The sun beat down on our heads and we tried not to panic as we started to feel very vulnerable.

Suddenly a small blue bird appeared on the ground in front of us. He cocked his head as if to say hello, and then hopped along between two trees. Then he came back to us and repeated the same actions. *Follow me,* I heard. Realizing he was there to help, we followed him. He hopped along and cocked his head repeatedly as if to make sure we were following, and before long we came to the Kachina Woman Rock. We were very relieved, and the bird disappeared as suddenly as he'd come. We stood and meditated in the vortex field of the rock, and the messages were wonderful, assuring us that things were going to work out. As the energy swept through us we felt transported back to an era when the Earth was worshipped and venerated and the area was peopled with noble races who should never have been driven out.

When the time came to leave, we had no idea how to find our way back to the car, but I called out with my mind to the little bird, who once again appeared and led us back to the part of the track that was well-worn enough to follow.

A Special Birthday Gift

For my thirtieth birthday Tony organized a rather special and unique surprise, which was to test my fearlessness and connection with animals in a wondrous and magical way. He wouldn't tell me where we were going until the actual day of the surprise, and even then all I knew was that we were going to Colchester Zoo, our local zoo at the time and renowned for its conservation programmes. Tony knew a secret desire I had. I was pretty obsessed with big cats, and ever since I was a child I'd wanted to get up close to some and try and communicate with them.

When we got to the zoo I was approached by a keeper, and the surprise was revealed. I was to accompany him on his rounds, and would be able to feed all the big cats. I was stunned. Any distaste I might have had for handling hunks of raw meat was totally eclipsed by the thrill of close contact with the cats. I was pretty amazed that the zoo was willing to let someone like me get so close to the wild animals. Even today, the more I think about it, the more bizarre it seems.

They started me off with the jackals, which I took to be a bit of a test – of my trust in the keeper, of my ability to follow his instructions, and of my nerve. I was sent in alone, a joint of meat in each hand, and told to crouch down, holding them at arm's length. The keeper told me the jackals would growl and snarl and run around me, but they wouldn't touch me, and I must show no fear. I could sense as they ran around me, growling, that they were afraid of me and just wanted their food, despite their bravado. After a few minutes they plucked up the courage to snatch the meat and run off with it. Next I graduated to a hyena, which was a bit bigger and a bit fiercer. I was told that, so long as I showed no fear, I would be safe. I felt no fear at all, as I could sense with all of these animals that all they were concerned about was getting fed.

After that it got really exciting, as in turn I fed a cheetah, a black panther, and the jaguars. Each of these was ordered (by me) to go into their 'houses', which they did, while I placed the meat strategically in their pens, and then released them again. Word seemed to get round because after a while, as soon as I approached the next pen the cats would immediately go into their houses without being told – well, not in words anyway.

The tigers and lions were an eye-opener, as this was the first time I'd ever been up close to one, and they were a lot bigger than they look from a distance. In the case of the lions, the procedure was a bit different. I went with the keeper behind the glass screen that separates the inner cages from the public. Then I was told to stick my hand, clutching a joint of meat, through a small panel in their cage wall, while the lions watched from their outdoor pen. The keeper held on to my arm because, he told me, the lions would come in extremely fast, and if I didn't pull my hand back in time, they were quite capable of getting their paw through the hole and ripping my arm off.

The male lion stunned me with the speed at which he leapt about 12 feet from a standing start, landing right inside the cage, and in a split second he'd grabbed the meat, as the keeper, with perfect timing, deftly whipped my hand away.

After that came what was the most thrilling part of the day for me. I was taken to the snow leopard's pen. These cats are incredibly beautiful, with their striking markings. I was instructed to go inside the safety pen and shut the door behind me before opening the door into his proper pen, where the snow leopard was lying on the ground, about ten feet from the door, waiting and watching. Were they really going to let me go into this cat's presence, unarmed, undefended and alone? Yes, they were. I'll never understand why I was allowed to do this. Even if the cat had been hand-reared, all big cats are still wild animals, and have been known to turn on their keepers in a flash. Even if the zoo carried public liability insurance, can you imagine any insurance company paying out in these circumstances? Public liability doesn't cover the risk of allowing a member of the public into a cage with a big cat!

Anyway, I was then told to go into the pen, holding the meat in front of me, and approach the cat, keeping full eye contact at all times. Then I was to place the meat about a yard in front of him and back out, still keeping eye contact. My heart was pounding with joy as I walked towards the snow leopard where he lay, and our eyes connected. I felt not a flicker of fear. The cat's eyes spoke to me, telling me I was quite safe, as I leaned down to place the meat at his feet. The absolute thrill of being so close to such a gorgeous wild animal, with no barrier between us, overrode every other emotion. I felt so privileged. This was probably the most 'in the moment' I'd ever been. It was a day I'll never forget.

Beachcombing

All through the years, my bond with animals has remained strong, and a major factor in my life. Once, Tony and I were walking along the beach in Great Yarmouth, in Norfolk, when we noticed some sort of fuss going on a little way ahead of us. As we reached the spot we saw that several young lads were standing in a circle, looking at something on the ground. Being curious, we stopped to see what was going on. A shag (a bird like a cormorant) was standing on the sand. The boys were throwing it bits of bacon, which it was gobbling down greedily. That was nice of them. The awful thing was that the bird was covered in oil. In that state it could not swim, fly or preen its feathers, and it certainly couldn't get any more food or, more importantly, water for itself. The boys told us they'd been keeping it alive for two days by feeding it scraps. I asked why they hadn't taken it to a rescue centre, because apart from anything else it would soon succumb to hypothermia with the oil all over it. They replied that they didn't like to try and pick it up in case it bit them. It *was* a fearsome-looking bird, it's true, about the size of a goose with a large, curved beak, and I didn't blame them for being wary, but the shag cried out to me for help.

I looked at Tony, and with a 'Here we go again' expression on his face he watched me walk up to the bird, pick it up and tuck it under my arm. I wasn't being brave. I knew it wouldn't bite because it had told me so, just as it had told me it wouldn't run or struggle. We took it to the coastguard station, and they phoned for a rescue centre to come and get it. At least the boys had cared, even if they hadn't really known the best thing to do!

We love to feed the birds here at our current home in Somerset, and we've counted over 30 species that visit our bird table. Occasionally we have a bird fly into our windows, despite the stickers all over them, and it falls to the ground, stunned. Each and every one is collected and put inside a warm box next to the oven to recover before being released. Left cold and still on the concrete, they'd soon die of shock or hypothermia, or become prey to a predator. We have rescued hedgehogs living in the garden, and in the time we've been living here we've stopped a pack of hounds from catching our resident fox, by standing between them and their prey and refusing to budge.

Encounters with Deer

Another time I got a message through animals was when we were walking KC, our dog, on the Quantock Hills. Tony was waiting for some quite serious hospital test results at the time, and I was hoping for some sort of sign that would help me feel secure about them. The Quantocks are an amazing spiritual place, and the energy is fantastic there. We were strolling along when some sixth sense made me turn around. I grabbed Tony's arm and turned him around, too. Filing past us, at a canter, was a whole herd of about 30 red deer. They were totally silent as they poured past, so silent that KC didn't even hear or see them, and she continued sniffing around in the grass as they passed us. The other strange thing apart from their silent passage was that, after they'd gone over the hill, we ran to the top (just a few yards) to watch them go and there was not a sign, no deer in sight, and not a single mark in the heather or gorse to mark their passing. I took this to be a good sign about the test results, and so it proved to be.

Just the other day, I was driving home up a steep hill. This road is full of sharp bends as well as being uphill all the way, so the tendency is to have your foot on the accelerator as much as possible, otherwise there's a chance your car won't make it. As usual I was rolling along taking the bends as fast as was safe, when suddenly I 'heard' the words, *I'm here, slow down*. I immediately slowed down to a crawl round the final bend, which was totally blind, and there, standing in the middle of the road, was a beautiful female roe deer.

If I'd been going any faster I'd have been unable to avoid hitting her, which would have been something I'd never have recovered from, I'm sure. I braked and stopped, and she didn't move at first, obviously unafraid, and our eyes met briefly through the windscreen of my car. I had time to admire her beautiful chestnut coat and her big black eyes, and then she tiptoed daintily across the road and slipped into the hedge at the side, vanishing silently in a few seconds.

Ace

Throughout my journey to spiritual enlightenment, I've had many other personal incidents that have convinced me that animals not only have souls but, in some ways, some of them are more spiritual than we are.

The biggest impact any experience with animals has had on me was with my dog, Ace. Ace was the closest an animal soul could ever get to a human soul. She was my shadow, and I loved her almost more than life.

When she died I was almost destroyed by grief, and the terrible need to know that she still existed somewhere, and was safe, ate away at me. I feel that sometimes the depth of our grief can 'block' a spirit, human or animal, from getting through to us. I think this is why manifestations or communications from those we have lost often don't come through for some time, perhaps not until after the grief has dulled a little.

Despite all my experience and the little messages I got from Ace, I needed another psychic person to bring me her most important message.

It was six months after she'd died, on 13th September, when a psychic in Arizona relayed a message to me from Ace, telling me that she was 'young again'. I didn't understand what this meant at first, but I came to realize that Ace was telling me she'd been reincarnated. But it wasn't until I met her again, and then saw a physical sign that she was the same dog, that I dared to really believe. Ace had undergone surgery when she was 12, which had entailed her losing a nipple, and the puppy, whom we called KC, was born with the same nipple missing, on the exact day (13th September) when the psychic got the message. After that I had yet another sign, when a psychic artist, June-Elleni Laine, drew an accurate portrait of the puppy which she said had come through to her from a black, German shepherd cross Labrador, which was exactly what breed Ace had been.

As well as sharing an important physical feature with Ace, there are many things KC just seems to know, from having been Ace in her previous life. For instance, one common area for accidents with any small animal under your feet is when you're carrying a container of anything hot. The chances of tripping over your pet are high. But Ace was badly scalded as a puppy (by her previous owners) by a kettle full of hot water, and KC will immediately get well out of the way, without being told, as soon as you pick up any container of anything hot, including a kettle, of which she's particularly wary.

KC also gave me one quite amusing sign that she was indeed Ace returned. In our garden we had a beautiful little rose tree that I planted over Ace's ashes. After blooming abundantly for several months, the rose tree suddenly died for no apparent reason. I was a bit upset, and left it in place for some time, hoping it would recover. After a while I saw the reason for the rose's demise. KC was urinating on it! This was out of character as KC is normally very well-behaved in the garden, never digs up plants and is always very circumspect in her toilet habits, always finding secluded and accepted areas to 'do her business'. At first, for a second, I was a bit annoyed, but then I was joyful again. KC was showing me that there was no need for a memorial to her previous self. She was back!

I also had an incredible, 20-year relationship with my Welsh cob horse, Sky. He was a very beautiful boy, of that there's no doubt, but he wasn't really what would be considered ideal, or natural, eventing material. Because of the speed, stamina and jumping ability required in the cross-country element, event horses are generally at least three-quarter thoroughbred – that is, bred to race. Being a Welsh cob, Sky was stocky, with high knee action (which slowed him down), a chunky body and not a huge amount of stamina. Nevertheless he had a huge heart and, most important of all, we understood each other. Despite all the odds, Sky scooted round the cross-country element of the events in a courageous and determined way, beating all the aristocratic thoroughbred horses on more than one occasion. His achievements amazed everyone, especially my competitors, and a lot of that was due to the fact that most of them were constantly misunderstanding what their horses were trying to tell them, whereas Sky and I were in constant communication. He was one in a million, and he taught me what a person and an animal together can achieve when they're a true team.

Chapter 1

Do Our Pets Have Souls?

'Who can believe that there is no soul behind those luminous eyes?'
— THEOPHILE GAUTIER

The word 'animal' comes from the Latin word *animale*, a form of the word *animalis* which in turn is derived from *anima*, which means 'vital breath' or 'soul'. The evidence I've uncovered during the writing of this book, as well as my personal experiences, have proved to me that animals do have souls. Just as it's ridiculous to think that people's personalities cease to exist when their mortal 'envelope' dies, it's untenable to think that animals, as noble as they are, don't exist after death, too.

Sceptics, even those who believe that people have souls, will argue that animals don't have souls because they're not self-aware. These sceptics will give the example that if you show an animal a reflection of itself in a mirror, it won't recognize what it's looking at. But they have to consider why it is that people *do* recognize themselves, and what purpose it holds for them. People look in a mirror for two reasons – to admire themselves or to try and change the way they look. This is vanity, and vanity is a completely alien concept to animals. Even a peacock, the most resplendent symbol of animal beauty, won't be in the slightest bit interested in finding a way to admire himself. He only cares if his display will attract a mate and deter rivals. Animals simply never consider how they look and they're not curious about it, so generally there's no point in them recognizing themselves in a mirror.

But I have a story that totally blows this sceptical argument out of the water anyway. While I was making one of my TV shows back in 2002, I was lucky enough to have a guest called Stella Marsden on the programme. Stella was part of the Chimpanzee Rehabilitation Trust, and sadly has now passed away. But during the filming she told me the story of one of her chimpanzees. This was a hand-reared chimp that lived in the house with the family, which included three women. This chimp was caught one day holding up a mirror and applying lipstick to its face. Of course it was imitating the women of the house, but it couldn't have applied the lipstick so accurately, and just to its lips, unless it had understood that it was looking at its own reflection in the mirror.

Sceptics will say that animals can't reason, but I've also owned dogs that could be asked a question such as 'We're going out. Do you want to go to the toilet before we go?' and have responded accurately to this question, either going to the door to be let out in the garden, or going straight to their bed, and they've never made a wrong call. This shows not only self-awareness, but also the ability to reason and to accept the consequences for their actions, something some humans have trouble with.

I've also heard people argue that animals can't have souls because you never hear of the ghosts of smaller or 'primitive' life forms. Whoever heard of a ghost ant or dinosaur, for instance? The answer to this lies in the theory of 'soul configuration'.

This theory states that a soul begins as a spark in the Earth, along with a myriad of other sparks, which together make up a whole soul. These new 'soul fragments' are blank, and whatever they experience in this form is brought, eventually, back to the whole, in order to subtly change it. This whole then fragments into another life form, such as a million blades of grass, all eventually bringing their experiences back into the whole, until eventually it has enough 'colour' to enable it to progress into the world of moving creatures. It may then become divided into 2,000 tadpoles, or 1,000 beetles or ants, and each part, as its physical shell dies, again brings new experiences back to the whole. This process continues up through the food chain, the whole soul finally dividing up into several mammals. It might be housed in a number of cows or sheep, for instance. Even our pets don't always have a whole soul – if they have you can easily tell, because they're the ones that seem 'almost human'. The ones that have an un-fragmented soul are the ones that are going to be human in their next incarnation.

This 'progression' of animal souls isn't meant to imply that humans are spiritually better than animals, just different. There are certain experiences that can only be gone through in the human condition, and these too must be lived through in order to ultimately produce a well-rounded, whole soul. In fact, only a soul that has become as spiritually attuned as an animal could possibly experience the emotional minefield of being a human and still have a chance of not being corrupted by it.

The 'soul configuration' theory also answers the question as to why there are no 'ghost ants' – because an ant contains only a tiny fraction of a soul, and therefore doesn't hang around after death; it's immediately absorbed back into the whole, so that the whole might move on. The same would apply to early life forms such as dinosaurs.

Another proof of animals having souls is when they show an awareness of, and an ability to help, other life forms, while putting themselves at risk; in other words, acting against their natural instincts for the sake of another being. Dolphins are a shining example of this. They don't naturally interact with man, have no apparent affinity with him, and they certainly don't owe him any debt of gratitude. And yet there are many stories of people who have been saved from drowning by the intervention of dolphins. Dolphins have even defended swimmers against their own natural enemies, sharks, thus putting their own safety in jeopardy.

My Life's Work

Since the day I realized that animals were actually communicating with me, and that it wasn't just that I loved them so, and felt for them, I've been helping people with their pets, especially dogs and horses. I can usually tell owners what's causing apparent 'misbehaviour' and get them back on track together. I also love to help all animals, including the wild ones that are hurt, trapped, abused or misused, in any way I can.

Animals have proven to me over and over again that they are sentient and, as such, that they must have souls. I've come across some incredibly touching and magical stories over the past few years. I've spoken to hundreds of people all over the world who are convinced their pet has a soul, and I've listened with ever-growing belief to their stories. If you've ever lost a much-loved pet, then the stories I've chosen to include here will lift your spirits and give you hope and comfort that your pet not only still exists after death, but may, in some cases, return to you, either in spirit or in a different body.

Chapter 2

Spirit Pets

This chapter is inevitably the longest in the book, because most spiritual pet experiences involve people communicating with their pet after it has died. Also, the most common pet ghosts are those of dogs, cats and horses, which confirms the theory that these are the animals whose souls are generally most advanced. This has also been the part of the book that has reduced me to tears most often, dealing as it does with the loss of much-loved pets. However, it's also been very uplifting, because the stories prove over and over again that our pets do still exist after death.

Dogs

'You think dogs will not be in heaven?
I tell you, they will be there long before any of us.'
– ROBERT LOUIS STEVENSON

I've chosen to put this story from Grace Knightly first because it so aptly demonstrates the courage and devotion that transcend death and are common to all much-loved dogs.

Like a lot of people and their pets, Jericho, my dog, was my baby. He meant the world to me. Also, like most people, I lived in dread of something happening to him, and me being helpless to do anything about it. My main fear as he got older was how I'd cope with the aftermath of his passing, even though I did believe in life after death, even for animals. He was one of those dogs that always wants to be with his owner, and I was afraid I was going to constantly wonder if he was OK, and if he'd found his way to wherever he was supposed to go, or whether he'd be wandering round in spirit, looking for me. I'd experienced losing my mum some years before, and I knew how awful I'd felt for months and months, wondering if she was all right, and never ever getting a sign to reassure me.

Jericho was a blue merle Border collie, with very unusual markings. Everyone commented on the lovely mixed colours in his coat. He was 11 years old when my fears came to life. One morning I called him to come and get in the car. I was a district nurse at the time, and he always went with me. If the patients wanted me to I'd bring him into their homes and they'd love petting him nearly as much as he enjoyed being petted. We lived on the Yorkshire Moors, so Jericho got enough glorious runs for ten dogs throughout the day. He loved going with me, and that was why a cold hand clutched at my heart when he didn't come running as usual. When he did appear he was obviously in pain. I won't go through the details of his illness, because it was too painful watching him go downhill to relive it.

Suffice to say that on a cold, grey day in March, Jericho and I took our last drive together in the car. Afterwards I drove back to the farm, where I lived with Dad, alone, crying and inconsolable. The empty seat beside me was like a cold, dark space. Jericho's body was wrapped in a plastic sack in the boot. When I got home we buried him in the yard, just where he'd have wanted to be.

That night I couldn't sleep, of course. I thought, *Here we go; this will be my life for the next few years*. Then I thought I heard a bark down in the yard outside my bedroom window. It sounded like Jericho, but there were three other dogs on the farm.

I heard the bark again. It really did sound like him, and I told myself I should go and check, whichever dog was barking. There might be something wrong.

I peered out of the kitchen door, and as I did the security light came on. That in itself was odd, because any previous movement in the yard, whether by dog or intruder, should have already triggered the light. I was blinded to the area for a minute and, as I walked forward clutching my dressing gown around me, I thought I could see a light on in my car.

It was very odd. At first I thought maybe I'd left one of the car doors slightly open, but the light had a strange luminescent quality I'd never seen before. I moved closer, peering into the car. Then suddenly there was a loud bang off to my left, and I jumped, startled. This was getting quite scary. I honestly thought about hightailing it back indoors, without even looking to see what the bang had been. When I did pluck up the courage to look, it wasn't anything I could have ever imagined. There was a sort of portal, an opening, surrounded by a corona of white light. The white light went back, slowly fading, into a tunnel. The thing it reminded me of was the white light and tunnel that I'd heard people who've experienced NDEs (near death experiences) describe.

What happened next was something I will never ever forget. A figure appeared in the distance, in the tunnel. As it came forward I could see it was a woman. Then my attention was switched back to the car, because I heard the door swing open. Revealed, enveloped in the unworldly white light, was … Jericho! He was sitting in the passenger seat, just like he always had done, just glowing.

A voice speaking to me dragged my eyes back to the tunnel. 'Gracie …' It was my mum's voice! And there she was, see-through and flickering, but standing in the entrance to the tunnel, unmistakably my mum.

'Oh God,' I muttered. Mum held up a hand as if to ward me off, 'Don't come over here,' she said, 'It's not your time, but it is Jericho's.' She pointed to the car. 'I don't want him to be stuck on Earth, following you round aimlessly. Tell him to come to me, Gracie.'

Shaking, absolutely enervated, I looked back. Jericho was sitting, staring studiously out through the windscreen, determinedly ignoring what was going on. I gaped.

'Gracie!' said Mum, 'Send him to me, before it's too late.'

Totally spaced out with emotion, I did as she asked. 'Jericho!' He looked at me guiltily, and tears filled my eyes, 'Come on, baby,' I said more gently, 'Come on, boy.'

Jericho slid out of the car and stood trembling on the ground, the white light having accompanied him. I wanted so much to go hug him, to go hug my mum, to do something other than stand there like an idiot while miracles were sprinkled around me.

Mum must have read my mind. 'Gracie!' she said in much the same tone I'd used on Jericho, 'Now, Gracie. There's no time!'

Not wanting my baby to be trapped on Earth, alone, I told him, 'Go to her, Jericho. You'll be safe with my mum.' I choked back tears as he walked slowly past me and over to the tunnel. My mum reached out and patted his head. My dog looked back at me one last time, and my mum, incredibly, waved, smiling. They turned and walked together into the light, into the tunnel, and with a softer, yet still startling snapping sound (a bit like an elastic band stretched and then let go), the tunnel vanished and there was just the cool empty night air, leaving me feeling like I'd just been sleepwalking. But I hadn't been.

This magical animal story achieves two objectives for me. One, it proves that the souls of our loved ones do wait for us on the other side, and two, that animals do go to heaven. How nice to know that your beloved pet is being cared for on the other side by your loved ones who have passed over!

Pauline Lee sent me the following lovely story about her dog, Pongo, who was obviously a very communicative and sensitive dog.

Way back in 1978 I went to the RSPCA kennels in Coventry to adopt a puppy. There were four small black bitches that had just been taken from their mother, and all were asleep. I put my hand into the box and chose the puppy that licked my fingers sleepily. I named her Pongo. She was six weeks old and a Labrador cross greyhound.

Pongo was a very intelligent girl who used to tug the hem of my skirt whenever my baby cried, just to let me know.

When Pongo was seven, we moved to Tamworth. I took my child to his new school on the first day and I didn't know anybody there at all, but suddenly Pongo pulled with all her might, dragging me over to a lady who stood by the gate. Pongo made a fuss of this lady, who told me that the previous day her old dog had died. It was almost as if Pongo knew and wanted to comfort her.

After Pongo died I was heartbroken. She was 16 years old by then and had been my best mate for all that time. My husband and older son took her to the vet for what, unbeknownst to me, was to be the last time. I was sitting on the sofa alone when I suddenly saw Pongo running across the room towards me, looking very young and happy, but she disappeared just before she reached me. I looked at the clock to see it was 5.30 p.m. When my husband and son came back with just a lead and collar, I knew. He said Pongo was put to sleep at exactly 5.30, so I believed she'd come to say goodbye to me.

I cried solidly for three weeks, but after that time we decided we should adopt another unwanted dog. We chose Misty. It was 16th February, and I asked Pongo to please send me some snow if she approved of our choice. Ten minutes later snow began to fall, although none had been forecast. Pongo used to sleep in her favourite spot under the stairs, so that was where we agreed to put Misty's bed. However, she wouldn't go under there at all but would just stare at the space with her ears up, whimpering. I knew

Pongo was reluctant to give up her bed, even in spirit, so I asked her to please let Misty into the bed, as she was only a puppy and needed comfort. Straight away Misty walked to the bed and lay down.

Lots of people have seen Pongo around the house since she passed over. One evening I heard her running up the stairs and felt her leap onto me as I lay in bed. I could feel her licking my face but couldn't move as she had pinned my arms down under the duvet. I asked her to get off, which she did. The dogs were never allowed upstairs in the bedrooms, but now she is in spirit she has no boundaries.

On another occasion I was having meat delivered by a butcher. It was a cold day and he stood with his back to the gas fire while he chatted. Next minute I was fascinated to see the tails of his white coat lift up. He shot around and said in a quivery voice, 'Now, tell me that was Misty,' but I said that Misty was actually asleep by the patio door. I knew it was Pongo. I don't know why but she found men's bottoms fascinating and would always have a sniff if she could. The butcher was pretty spooked, as he said he'd felt a dog's head lift up the bottom of his jacket.

Misty's in spirit now, and like Pongo she frequently visits us. Misty has also jumped on the bed, which she used to do when she was younger, but she always used to lie at my feet, whereas Pongo would try to get as close to my face as she could. So I know which one is visiting me and

I always move my legs over when I hear one of them run up the stairs, so that they have room to lie down.

Another story that happened while Pongo was still alive, involves Pippa, a friend's beagle. Pippa used to come with her owner each Friday for a cup of coffee and a biscuit. Pippa got on really well with Pongo and the dogs would happily play together. One day my friend told me that Pippa had been diagnosed with leukaemia and couldn't walk too far any more. However, they still came to our house on a Friday, and Pongo would bring one of her chews and place it before her friend. Pippa couldn't manage to eat it – but the thought was there.

The following week my family and I went on our fortnight's holiday. When I got back I discovered that Pippa had died in our absence. On the Friday that she'd died, earlier in the day she'd disappeared. Her owner had searched everywhere, and eventually found her sitting outside my front door. My friend took her home, and that night she passed away. We both believe that Pippa came to say goodbye to us all.

That beautiful story showed not only a dog's very real connection to her owner, but also to another dog. It also showed that a dog can know and understand when it's going to die. So much for dogs not being self-aware!

Here is another story, from June-Elleni Laine, which shows how dogs are sometimes so loyal that they won't even let death relieve them of their duty.

Rocky was my gorgeous white boxer dog, my faithful friend for five years. Then one awful day when he was eight he was diagnosed with an inoperable tumour on his heart, and I knew it would be only a matter of time before I'd have to make the dreadful decision to let him go. I spoke to Rocky and explained that our time together had almost come to an end and that I'd do my very best to make his last few weeks or maybe months as pleasant as I could. I vowed that I wouldn't let him suffer, and that when I felt his quality of life wasn't acceptable I'd send him into the spirit world, where we could meet again when my time was over. I felt he knew, as if this was a decision we'd somehow agreed upon even before I'd adopted him as a rescue dog. He'd stayed with me through very vulnerable times in my life and now I was stronger, his job was almost done. We both knew, and on a deep level accepted, what had happened.

One morning I looked at him and I could 'see' his skull showing through his face. I knew it was time, and that the dreaded day had arrived. The inner voice began its vocal accusations. I tormented myself with questions. Had I left it too long? Was he suffering too much? Was I being selfish? But then the inner knowing kicked in and assured me that I'd kept my end of the deal. That day was indeed the right time.

I fed him a steak and even let him have a slurp of wine, as it was the last meal he'd have in this dimension. I took him for one last walk in the park beside the vet's surgery, and when the appointed time was upon us, I gave him a big hug. Caught up in my own grief, I just told him we were going to the vet's and that he was going to go to sleep. He accepted calmly, as he always had done through all the examinations, injections and X-rays he'd been through before. As the vet administered the fatal injection, my heart broke and I screamed out in pain. I was left hugging Rocky's limp body until I couldn't cry any more. I left 30 minutes later, resolving that I would smile because of the time I'd been given with him, and not cry because it was over. I'd celebrate the time we had and be glad he was no longer in discomfort – but that was easier said than done! For the next week I felt him following me around, but put it down to my imagination. Even when I was in a restaurant having dinner, I thought I saw him waiting outside by the door. Again I put this down to wishful thinking on my part.

Then one night I was proved wrong. I woke up suddenly, thinking, *Oh my God, I can't breathe!*

I staggered out of bed, panicking, and rushed for the window as I felt my chest fighting to expand enough to draw in a breath. I felt dizzy as I struggled to open the window. With my head hanging outside and the cold night air blowing directly into my face, I still couldn't breathe deeply. It was horrible, as if my worst nightmare was continuing even though I was wide awake. Gradually the palpitations decreased, breath returned and I begun to feel calmer.

What on Earth had happened?

I suddenly realized that Rocky was there. He didn't know what had happened to him, and he didn't want to leave me. I hadn't said goodbye to him properly. I'd picked up the symptoms of his heart problems as he'd jumped onto the bed and lay beside me in his spirit body that night.

That breathless encounter convinced me that Rocky was indeed still there, waiting for me to explain what had happened, and to say goodbye. Now I'd experienced for myself how uncomfortable it had been for him towards the end, but at least I knew for sure then that I'd made the right decision in letting him go. After I got my breath back and closed the window that night, I calmly explained to Rocky's spirit that I'd asked the vet to end his life in the body that was causing him such pain, and that I'd always love him. I told him that now he could move into another dimension, where he'd be free of discomfort. He could go to a place without the limitations of the physical plane, and somewhere I'd be with him again at the right time. And maybe, just maybe, part of me was already there, waiting for him.

He seemed to understand what I said, and a golden light began to fill the room. As it reached a peak and then slowly faded, I suddenly felt happy that the chapter was complete and that Rocky was free to be. This was such proof for me that our pets do have spirit bodies and that their consciousness does survive death of the physical body. I'm convinced Rocky and I are soulmates, and that we'll always have a loving connection.

So poor Rocky was so determined to stay by his mistress that he didn't even know he was dead. He was still suffering the symptoms of his illness because he hadn't been released from his guard post. Thank goodness his owner was able to understand what was going on and let his spirit as well as his body go.

Alice Jean has lived a wonderful life full of connections to her dogs, goats and other animals. This is one of her stories.

Last time we were in Ireland, my brother took my hubby and me to a pub for lunch. All three of us sat right inside the door, facing the next room where there was a pool table. I could see two large Labs asleep under the pool table. After about two minutes each dog popped up its head and trotted towards us. I was sitting in the middle between my hubby and my brother. Both dogs were trying to get to me, almost pushing my hubby's chair out from under him! My brother, Gene, was laughing his head off as he got up and moved out of the way, all the while explaining to my hubby that this kind of thing had been going on all our lives and that his sister seems to attract the animals. Turning to me, he quickly added that that was a compliment!

As a child I never heard anyone warn me not to look animals right in the eyes, like I hear these days, so I never knew better! I always looked into their faces and wondered what they were thinking and feeling. I've always loved them, pets and wild ones, too. Probably anyone who has lived with any kind of animal has to wonder about what animals think and feel. What do they know that we haven't a clue of? I feel like I was given one answer the day my dear Laban died. He was a huge Great Pyrenees dog that lived with my dairy goats, and was my dear pal. We hadn't a clue that he was sick, or even feeling bad in any way. I had a long pipe-feeder over my head one day, trying to make my way through the many goats crowded around me without tripping. I felt Laban lean against my legs for a moment, like he did sometimes. 'Oops, move, pup,' I said, as I made my way to the fence to rest that feeder on the ground. I looked back at him, and went and gave him a pat on the head and headed out. I went to the little store just down the road for ice cream, and was back in minutes. When I got back I noticed that the goats were gathered around something in a circle in the pasture. All I could see were goat backsides, so I walked out there. Before I got anywhere close to them they had decided to slowly walk off. There on the ground lay Laban. He was dead. The vet thinks his heart just gave out.

Do I think the goats were honouring him? Yes, I do. Do I think they loved him as much as he loved all of them? Yes, I do. For three days everyone in the barn was very quiet. Nubian goats are not normally known to be the quiet kind. Of course I cried my eyes out for three days. Then we all went on. I still miss him.

Nelson was a Great Pyrenees male given to me when he was three years old. I hesitated about taking him because the woman who made this gift told me that she had never really bonded with him. She liked another of her dogs better and paid no attention to Nelson. Besides, if I wanted another livestock guard, I wanted to get it at five to six weeks old, not three years old! I needed that dog to be bonded to me and my goats, like Laban had been. The reason we chose the Great Pyrenees over other breeds of livestock guard dogs is for their wonderful gentle temperament. I'd never be afraid to send my little grandchildren out there with them. They look like big lazy goofs during the day, but that's deceiving because they'll give their life to defend the ones they love. Nelson had never had a collar on, and had never been told what to do. He and I had a 'stand-off' one day, right after we brought him home, when he wanted to go into a yard I didn't want him in. He actually growled at me! I never, in all my life, had a dog growl at me! It scared me a little, but mostly I knew I had to fix this! I couldn't live with a dog that was bigger than me and thought he was my boss! I walked into the barn and got a collar and leash and quickly put it on him, all the while shaking my finger in his face and telling him that I was boss, and wondering if my finger would be bitten off! He didn't argue with me at all. I didn't even speak to him the rest of the day, which my husband thought was a little cruel on my part. It worked, though. The next day Nelson did everything he could, which included acting goofy and flopping over on the ground at my feet, to make up for his bad behaviour. We loved each other for many years after that, Nelson and I. Then one day I asked him if he were willing to live with this family he'd seen many times, and make puppies. He loved the children in that family, so I knew he'd be happy with them. They'd lost their male dog, and loved Nelson. He sat up straight and put his head up for a collar and lead, and walked like a little prince out to their truck. I was so proud of him and he knew it. They brought me one of his pups, and that dog lives with me now. One day standing at the kitchen sink, and off in a trance as usual, I saw Nelson lying there on the hill in the pasture, head up, looking around. Suddenly I realized that Nelson didn't live with us any more. The next day I called the people who had him. They told me that they were planning on coming to tell us that Nelson had died during the storm we'd had, maybe struck by lightning! I know he wanted me to see him, here at home again. I think he's always around.

June Bailey's story follows. This is the tale of two dogs – one who took his watchdog duties very seriously, even after he'd died, and of the great connection her other dog had to her, which meant she felt her pet's death even though she was miles away at the time.

I can remember the day Rover came into my life as if it was yesterday, although I was only six years old at the time. My dad rescued him from a boy who'd been about to drown him. He was a Border collie with a black-and-white coat. I was at exactly the right age to have a dog, and I always felt so safe with Rover at my side. I loved him to bits, and he wouldn't let anyone harm me. He would even watch over me protectively if my mum was telling me off for something. He wasn't a particularly healthy dog, though, I suppose because of his bad start in life, and by the time he was nine he was going downhill fast.

He started getting lumps on his body, and his back legs went, so he couldn't walk on his own. I still loved him very much and, despite his heaviness, I'd carry him around the house, outside to do his business, and then at night upstairs to bed. I thought we were doing all right, but of course my parents knew the end was in sight for Rover. He couldn't be allowed to carry on suffering that way. When dogs can't do normal 'doggie' things, they aren't happy. My dad was off work as he'd a slipped disc, and so money was very tight at that time.

As soon as they had enough money for the vet, one morning my parents waited until I went off to school, and when I came home that day my precious friend was gone. My mum and dad had loved Rover, too, and the three of us cried and cried together. When I went to bed that night the bed felt so empty without him at first, but then I pulled my pillow down the bed as I always had, to make room for Rover at the top, and I felt that he was still there with me.

The next morning I set off for school and thought about Rover with every step. Suddenly I could hear a clicking noise, and I finally realized that with every step I took there was the sound of claws on the pavement keeping up with me. Rover was trotting alongside me, keeping watch on me, just as he always had when he was well. This continued, every day, for nearly two years, until we were ready to get another dog.

This was another Border collie, and she was like a negative of Rover. She had the same markings, but she was white where he'd been black, and black were he'd been white. I named her Sheba because it was like the name was shouted in my head, and I knew it was her name. My dad was very strict with our dogs, in as much as he would never let them out in the street, except only with him, and only on a leash. They were only allowed to run free in an open field where there was no danger from traffic.

Sheba and I had a close connection. I was 18 by then, and sometimes felt down, as teenagers do. Sheba would understand how I was feeling when it seemed no one else did, and she would nuzzle up close to me, licking my tears away.

Tragedy struck when Sheba was just four years old. It wasn't like her, but for some reason that day she jumped the fence into a neighbour's garden and ran off. I didn't know about it, as I'd already gone to work. Maybe she was trying to find me. I'll never know for sure.

I suddenly got this awful feeling deep in my stomach. I didn't know what it was, but I knew I had to go home immediately, so I told my staff supervisor that I was ill and had to go home. As soon as I got into the house and my lovely Sheba wasn't there to greet me like she always did, I knew. My mum told me that Sheba had been knocked over by a car and killed, while running away from another dog. The man that had knocked her over had lifted her to the side of the road and gone into our local police station to report it. They had called Mum to tell her. What was odd was that the accident happened at exactly the same time I felt sick and said I had to go home. It was like Sheba was calling out to me to say goodbye.

Bev Wilson's story started off as quite scary, though it soon became clear there was nothing to fear from this particular doggy spirit.

When I moved into my new home I was very happy. It was just an old terraced mill cottage, but to me it was home sweet home, a veritable castle. After being in rented places for so long, I finally had my own front door. That first night I slept like the dead, I was so tired, having moved in single-handed. But the next night it was different. I woke up. It was dark and I had no idea what had woken me. Then I heard it, a distinct thump, thump, thump. I had no stair carpet at the time and it sounded just like footsteps jogging really heavily down the stairs. My first thought was, *Burglar!* I was a woman alone in the house, but then I thought that the walls weren't that thick and I knew I had neighbours on either side, so that if I screamed someone would be bound to hear me and call the police. I must have been more tired than I thought, because the next thing I knew it was morning. I forgot all about what I presumed had been a dream.

The next night it happened again, only worse. It started with the sound of light footsteps coming close to my bedroom door. For a moment I was sure that something was going to come into the bedroom. The footsteps were quick and not very loud, and sounded stealthy, but the next noise wasn't subtle at all. It was the thumping noise again, and my heart echoed the thump, thump, thump. I knew I was wide awake and not dreaming. Then an even scarier noise – chains rattling. Now, I was well into new-age stuff and I couldn't believe that if this was going to turn out to be a ghost, it was going to manifest in such a clichéd way as with chains rattling. Besides, this wasn't the Tower of London – it was an ordinary terraced cottage! I hid under the covers, telling myself it would go away if I didn't respond to it. It didn't. It happened every night. Finally, more exhausted than I'd ever been, I decided to call in a medium.

Of all the things I might have expected her to come up with, she told me the noises were being caused by the ghost of a dog! She told me that a big golden retriever that used to live in the house was making all that noise! The muffled footsteps were actually 'paw-steps', the thumping was him dropping his ball down the stairs. And the chains? That was him taking his lead in his mouth and shaking it from side to side!

The dog told the medium that during his lifetime in the house I was living in, he had often been locked in a big cupboard under the stairs while the owners were out. He'd died in that cupboard. The poor dog had been waiting for years and years for somebody who was 'open' to live in the house, so that he could use their energy to manifest himself. The dog told her that if he could be allowed to stay for a few more days, he would be ready to leave. Sure enough, true to his word, three days later the dog visited for the last time, and I never heard from him again. I was able to confirm with neighbours, though, that the previous owners had once had a big golden retriever.

This is a strange one, as the dog didn't know the person who heard him. Poor thing must have been waiting for years until the right person came into the house to let him manifest himself, even if only by sound. I'm sure that in heaven there would have been many balls for him to play with, but it seems it was very important to him that he played with that particular ball, because he was denied it in life.

The very fact that a dog can have 'unfinished business' on Earth in just the same way that a person can is more proof that we and our pet and animal companions are much closer spiritually than a lot of people think.

Lynn Kilpatrick was close enough to her dog that she knew he'd passed away, even though nobody else did.

When I was 17 years old, our pet American cocker spaniel, Sandy, had a heart attack. I was deeply upset about Sandy being ill, especially as earlier we'd left him alone in his basket and had all gone up to bed. I couldn't rest, though, as somehow I knew that he was going to be leaving us, and I lay in bed crying and listening to Spandau Ballet on my little cassette player.

As I lay there with tears streaming down my cheeks, soaking my pillow, I suddenly saw Rover and Royce, our old dogs, in my room, followed by Sandy. I knew then that he'd died, and went running into my mum's room saying I was very thirsty and needed a glass of water. I asked her if she would go and get me one. One look at my face told her that I knew Sandy had died, so she agreed to go into the kitchen to get my glass of water. She went downstairs and a minute later called up to me to get my eldest sister up. I went and got my sister, who went down. I could hear them talking together and some movement before they came back upstairs. Sandy had indeed died in his sleep in the kitchen.

This story was sent to me by Hazel Chubb. It demonstrates yet again the inventiveness of pets when it comes to leaving a physical sign that they're still with us.

Millie, our Maltese terrier, was the most beautiful little dog, and so smart. She knew every word we were saying and could communicate 'yes' and 'no'. She would nod and sneeze for 'yes', and give a shake of her head for 'no'. She'd do her 'Bob-a-job' work, as we'd call it: we'd get her to pick up washcloths and other small items for the laundry basket and carry them in her mouth to the basket or the washing machine.

Once the job was done, she'd get her treat. My dad also taught her to bring her plastic dish for a cup of coffee. He got down on the floor with the dish in his mouth and crawled round the floor to show her how to carry it. Mind you, if Mum gave her a drop of tea instead of coffee, she'd upend the dish on the floor because it wasn't coffee. I guess she was more than a little bit spoiled. We wouldn't allow Dad to put a kennel outside for her and she was very much an inside family dog all her life. Dad and my sister would often tease her and ask her to 'Show us your teeth,' so she did. She'd bare her teeth and growl. Some of her 'human antics' were great.

She was named Millicent by my dad, but that quickly got changed to Millie for short. She was only called Millicent when she was in trouble. Her nickname was Mim, which also came from my dad. I think she really understood everything we said to her, and she was such a loyal pet that one time when my mum took her for a walk and fell over on the way, Millie took off and started running for home to get help. Fortunately Mum was able to pick herself up and stop Millie from running all the way home.

Our Millie died in September last year, and every so often she visits us. She leaves behind little tufts of white fur that

I find on the floor, usually near the sliding door she used to use to go out into the back garden, and I'm convinced that it's her way of letting me know she's around. We bought a new puppy in January this year, a cavalier King Charles spaniel we call Lady, and she sometimes looks straight at Millie's picture on the wall and barks, and I'm certain she sees Millie sometimes. I've also seen a small white light darting across the kitchen early in the morning around breakfast time.

My dog, Ace, once made her rose, planted as a memorial to her, glow with such heat that normally the flower would have shrivelled and died. We'd felt just like we were standing round a heater.

Kathleen Janssen sent me this simple but beautiful little story about Ubu and her rose. I've seen a photo of this unusually bred little dog, and she really was unforgettable.

It was a cold winter day but the roads had thawed for the first time in a week. Enough so we were able to drive to the nearest grocery store for provisions. We had no intention of coming home with a pup, but then we saw two young children with a box of blue-eyed puppies. We didn't care about gender when we got Ubu, as we were rescuing her, and she was the least attractive. We figured the others would find other homes as they had pretty markings. The children told us the pups' mother was a blue heeler and the father an Irish terrier. I carried her home, cuddled against my body inside my shirt. She was such an odd-looking animal that when my daughter saw her peeking out of my jacket she exclaimed, 'What is it?' Ubu would never win any beauty contests but her loyal devotion made her a winner in our eyes. We had her for 17 wonderful years, and even towards the end she would do her best to stand guard, even though she was old and frail. Just when I was thinking that I'd have to make the awful decision to let her go, one hot day Ubu passed away quietly at home. It was as if she wanted to make it easier for me. We buried her in the backyard under the ponderosa pine we brought from the old house when Ubu was just two years old. Then we went out and got a rose bush to mark her resting place. I went through the day feeling that the world seemed so different without her. She had been with us for so long. I'd been thinking, too, about what a psychic had told me about how Ubu's final moments would be. And now, looking back at all that happened, I see how everything fell into place for us to be together at that time. I had hoped that she would pass peacefully in her sleep but I'd wanted to be with her. I didn't think it would be likely that that would happen, but it did. On that day I was meant to go on a shopping trip with my daughter, but a strange thing happened with our communications and she left without me. It was very odd that

that had happened. If all had gone as planned I would have been gone and missed Ubu leaving. She was also so faithful to her job watching over us that I had hoped she'd be able to work up to the end, and she did. I'm looking forward to meeting that sweet soul again someday. Oh yes ... the rose we got is called Oranges and Lemons. The flower is striped two-toned. It's unique, just like Ubu. The rose didn't have any flowers until my birthday in July, and then there it was – one perfect bloom – a gift from my wonderful and amazing dog, Ubu.

Karen Jones had this amazing experience quite out of the blue, when she was least expecting it. It goes to show that animals will connect with you quite naturally if you're just open enough to accept communication. This openness is one of the keys to communicating with your pet, living or in spirit.

I've always been open to spirits, and seen more than a few inexplicable things in my life, but this one had me flummoxed. I was on my way to a party one evening, on foot as it was at a neighbour's house, when I suddenly realized that a little dog was tracking me along the other side of the road. It was a tiny little thing, a chocolate-coloured toy poodle, and I didn't really think it should have been out alone, but the housing estate was quiet at that time of day and the dog didn't seem to be in any distress, just trotting along, glancing across at me now and again as if to make sure I was still there. I stopped to talk to a friend outside her house and the dog carried on on its way, as if it knew where it was going, so I forgot about it.

Minutes later when I went around the next corner, there was the same dog again. Just as if it had been waiting for me, it was sitting at the kerbside. When I got close, up it got and on it went again, always in the same direction as me. I went past a small shopping arcade and decided to pop into the off-licence for a bottle of wine to take with me to the party. When I came out the dog had gone again. I carried on and this time I was watching out for it, but I didn't see it. Then I reached the party address, and as I turned to walk up the garden path I caught a glimpse of movement out of the corner of my eye. I looked ahead, further up the road, and there was the same dog again. It was about 50 feet away and sitting staring across at me from the other side of the road. I decided to put an end to the mystery and go and have a proper look at the dog. To come out of the garden I had to pass behind a big buddleia bush, and when I got to the street the dog had gone again. I couldn't understand it as there didn't seem to be anywhere it could have gone.

I shrugged and went into the party. I started chatting to my host, and she told me that the whole family had almost decided to call the party off as they weren't in a celebrating mood. They'd only gone ahead because none of the family could bear the thought of trying to call all the guests and put them off. Besides, they thought a party would take their minds off what had happened. I asked what that was, of course. She went on to tell me that their little toy poodle, Fancy, had escaped from the garden that morning and had been hit by a car a few streets away – right along the route I'd taken to walk there. I was staggered. This was the first time I'd been to their house, and hadn't even known they had a dog. I was even more staggered when she went on to describe the dog, which matched exactly the one I'd seen.

I persuaded her to go outside with me, thinking she might see the dog, but there was no sign of it. I had no option really but to tell her what I'd seen. She burst into tears, luckily happy ones, and rushed me back in to tell the rest of the family. It was great, as I quickly became the hero of the party. But I'm still puzzled as to why the dog appeared to me instead of to its owners, as surely that would have been of more comfort to them?

I think that spirits, whether human or animal, need the right sort of energy to manifest. This is why some people will never see a ghost, even if they're surrounded by them. It's also why some people will always need mediums in order to connect with passed-over souls.

The following story came to me from Marshall McDaniel in Canada. It's a touching 'boy and his dog' story, and Bear, the dog, certainly had a novel and appropriate way of making his presence felt.

Bear and I grew up together. He was a black Labrador puppy, and when he arrived I was a baby. My parents told me that from the day I was born, Bear would lay by my crib while I slept, let them know when I was awake and oversee my baths, like some kind of canine nanny. As soon as I started moving under my own steam, scooting round the house on my hands and knees, Bear would be right behind me, trying his best to stop me getting hurt by grabbing my clothes and steering me away from anything dangerous. Bear was my best friend, and as we grew up we got ever closer. I had a tough time at school, being picked on because of my Christian upbringing. It was a rough area and I often came home from school bloodied and bruised. When I got home Bear would be waiting and he'd lick me and curl around me, trying to take the hurt away. One funny thing, though: my brother was born after me, but Bear didn't want anything to do with the new baby. He was just 'my dog' and that was all there was to it.

Life was so much better with my big buddy, and he made me feel special and needed, when I didn't ordinarily feel that way. When you're a kid it's hard to imagine people and animals leaving you, getting sick and dying, and maybe that's for the best. I had no premonition, but on my tenth birthday, right in the middle of my party, Bear started acting weird. He was puffing and panting, and foam gathered around his mouth, dripping to the floor. He was jerking around, too. Because I was only ten I didn't understand what was happening to my friend, although now I know that he was actually having serious convulsions. Of course my dad knew what was going on, so he told my mom to take the kids home and meet him at the vet's. Then he scooped Bear up and put him in the truck, and I went with him. I'm shaking now, recalling how I felt on that drive, when I looked down at my buddy's apparently lifeless body. His eyes were glazing over and I was very scared I was going to lose him.

The vet did some tests and some X-rays and told us we had to leave Bear with him overnight. It felt so wrong going home without him. The truck was silent and I thought that was one of the worst things about being just a kid – you didn't get to make decisions. I would have rather my dad had left me at the vet's with Bear. I would have slept better there just feeling his breathing body tucked up to mine. I didn't sleep at all in my bed.

First thing in the morning we rushed to the vet's to find out the news. They told my parents that poor Bear had a brain tumour and it was causing internal bleeding on his brain. They would, they said, do what they could to help him. They did do their best, but during the longest week of my life Bear deteriorated and the vet said he might as well go home. I wasn't told what was wrong with him, and all I knew was that Bear was coming home. I was totally stoked about it. Sure, I could see he was still sick, but I thought he'd be better at home with me to care for him. He lay in the yard on a blanket and I lay down next to him. I remember saying, 'No matter what happens, I'll always love you.' I was so happy that I was bonding with him again.

I went to bed that night feeling better than I had all week, but the next morning when I rushed down to see him, Bear's bed was empty. It was the worst day of my life. When my mom told me Dad had taken Bear to the vet's again, and tried to explain gently that my buddy was never coming home, I just collapsed. I'd thought I'd got him back, and now he'd been snatched away again. I couldn't believe it, but it was true. Dad brought home his ashes. That was all that was left of my best friend, just a pile of ashes. It was surreal. We buried them with his favourite bone, and planted a little tree there. I put a bunch of flowers on the grave.

I lay awake that night, crying. I was heartbroken, abso-lutely heartbroken. I got up and went down to the kitchen, supposedly to get a cup of water, but I was just looking, searching for something to cling to. When I turned on the light I didn't want to see Bear's empty bed, still where I'd last seen him alive, but I had to look, and I gasped, because there he was. Well, his spirit anyway. Bear had a bone in his mouth, the same bone we'd buried with his ashes. He was wagging his tail and looking really happy. I didn't know whether to laugh or cry. It was impossible, but it was true. Bear dropped the bone, but it fell silently, not making a sound as it hit the floor. He gave it a little shove with his nose, as if to say, 'Come on! Play with me, buddy!' I walked over and went to grab the bone, but then he and the bone disappeared. I fell to my knees and broke down, sobbing. My mom and dad heard me and came rushing into the kitchen to comfort me. They let me sleep in their room for the rest of the night.

Every once in a while, it doesn't matter which house I'm living in, I'll sometimes see Bear, just out of reach, wagging his tail, just telling me that he's still there and that we'll be reunited again one day. Writing this story down was really hard for me. It's hard losing a pet ... especially when you've become so close.

Pets and spirits of all kinds, that come through clearly enough to be seen, expend a great deal of energy, so you know it's very important to them that their grieving owner should be comforted by them. Bear obviously loved Marshall a great deal. I'd be willing to bet that he turns up again later in Marshall's life, in another body.

Cats

'I have studied many philosophers and many cats.
The wisdom of cats is infinitely superior'

— HIPPOLYTE TAINE

Cats seem to appear just as often as dogs, which might seem a bit strange as they're often a lot more aloof and independent than dogs, but we have to remember that that's just because of the body and personality that they're in. Underneath they're just as attached, spiritually, as any other being.

This next beautiful story, about Oscar, came to me from Ross Gatty.

Oscar always liked men better than women, but he was a very shy cat with strangers. A black-and-white tuxedo-wearing cat (just like the cartoon cat, Felix), he had a very sweet nature and loved to show his affection to me and my late dad. I was devastated when Oscar got sick, aged about ten – young for a cat – and the very bad news was that he had an inoperable stomach tumour. The vet did his best, but could really only postpone the inevitable with painkillers.

Eventually the dreaded day came. I'd spent the night before with Oscar and he'd seemed quite serene, almost as if he knew and was quite happy about it. He was put on a drip at the vet's so he was in no pain and, happily for us both, he passed away peacefully during the next night. I really loved that cat, and although some people might say, he was 'just a cat', to me he was a gentleman and a very good friend. Oscar never judged me or fell out with me, and he was a faithful buddy.

A few months later, Oscar paid me a visit. It was as if he was proving to me that he had no hard feelings and was still faithful. I'd just woken up and was still lying in bed, face down. I felt the bed spring slightly as something fairly light jumped onto the bottom. Then I felt very slight, ethereal footfalls going up, all the way up and along my back, and then a weight settled down next to the pillow, right by my head. I felt something touch my head, which could have been a paw nudge, or a sniff or a huff of breath. Then the weight moved away and got off the bed, without making a sound. It struck me then that this was just what Oscar used to do, exactly what Oscar used to do in the mornings.

I threw back the covers and jumped out of bed to see if any of our other three cats were in the room, but the door was shut fast and there were no cats to be seen. I think this was Oscar, and I think he came to say goodbye, because that had been my only regret, that I hadn't been with him when he died. I believe that cats and all animals have souls, and it's just that science hasn't yet found a way to register them.

Oscar chose the route of doing what he'd always done to make his presence known. If this had been a vision rather than a touch sensation, you might ask if this was a 'recording' of energy replaying itself, rather than a new manifestation, but in this case Ross says the feeling of Oscar's paws was unmistakable.

Jamie Kiffel is one of the editors of a mainstream magazine in the USA, and I was delighted that she chose to share her story with me.

Sam, a striking, all-black American shorthair, was our beloved cat for 21 years. After I grew up and moved out, he continued to live with my mom and dad, but whenever I visited Sam would come running, meowing to greet me and wanting me to pick him up and carry him around. He was closer still to my dad and watching them together it was almost more like a man and his dog than a man and his cat. Mom sometimes felt a bit left out because when we were in the room Sam's attention almost always turned to me and Dad. Yet in the afternoons when she came home from work to watch her soap operas and neither of us was around, Sam would always curl up next to her and give the impression that he was watching TV too.

Sam was a very healthy cat all his life, and it wasn't until his final week that he started to slow down. Up until then, guests never believed he was an old cat, although it wasn't hard to tell that he was an old soul. When he got a bit doddery, we took him to the vet's for a check-up, and it was right there, on the vet's table that Sam had a stroke and, with the grace and dignity he'd always had, passed on. We were heartbroken, and we missed him so much. Still, Mom was just a bit wistful to think that we'd had a closer connection to him than she'd had. A few weeks after Sam's death I had an amazing dream. I dreamed that I was in a mansion and my dad and Sam were there. Also there was Cherokee, Sam's sister cat who'd died about six years previously. Cherokee looked the same as always, meowing and seeming very happy, but Sam had changed somehow. I realized that he was trying to speak words, and he did just that, forming them very slowly as if his cat mouth and vocal cords were causing him a problem. 'Ask them,' he said to me, and I knew he meant my parents, 'why they're still hanging that hat over there.' Dad, in the dream, said, 'Tell him that's OK. We're sorting it out.' Then Sam said, 'Tell her,' meaning my mom, 'I saw how she arranged the pictures of the children. She did a great job, and I'm so proud of her.' After the dream I immediately called my parents and related the whole thing to them. My dad explained that my mom was dithering with changing her job, and he figured that the reference to the hat meant they had to stop 'hanging their hat' on her old job. But it was my mom who really surprised me. She laughed and said, lightly, 'That's nice. When you come over, I'll show you the pictures of the children.'

'What pictures?' I asked. 'I don't know about any pictures.' Mom realized then that she'd never mentioned the pictures to me. Stunned, she told me that she'd been working hard each night on assembling photo albums of the children at the local school where she'd worked. I was astounded, and I told her, 'You see, you always worried that you didn't have as close a connection to Sam as we did, and now you know you did. He went to all that trouble to prove it to you.' I've no doubt that this really was Sam in the dream, because how else could I have dreamed accurately about something that I'd known nothing about?

Rachael Doonar-Nix wrote from Australia to tell me this short but sweet little tale of Floyd, the cat.

One terrible day our cat, Floyd, was killed by a car, but I had no idea it had happened until later. Before I'd even noticed he was missing, my then five-year-old daughter came out to me looking very startled, saying that she'd seen Floyd walk right through the wall into the laundry room, and then she'd seen him jump through and into the washing machine. She was very upset and scared he would be 'washed' and hurt if we didn't get him out. I went into the laundry room but couldn't find him. It occurred to me I hadn't seen him all day and we went searching for him. We found poor Floyd lying dead on the side of the road.

It's always good when a child sees a spirit because they don't try and rationalize or explain away what they're seeing. To a child the world is already full of magical things they don't understand, so when they have a paranormal experience they just tell it like it is, and their evidence is therefore very compelling. You have to wonder if Floyd chose to appear to the child because of this.

Horses

'To understand the soul of a horse is the closest human beings can come to knowing perfection.'

– ANONYMOUS

Horses might not live in our homes with us, but people who own horses generally have just as close a relationship as others do with dogs and cats that share their home, because of the unique companionship that has always existed between man and horses throughout history. Man has dragged horses into war for centuries, and submitted them to horrendous injuries and death, in a conflict the horses themselves could never comprehend, and they have obeyed just because their rider wanted them to. So it's no wonder horses are considered just as noble as the pets we invite into our own homes.

This applies especially nowadays to competition horses, because this partnership is one of the best examples there is of animal and man cooperating in perfect harmony and understanding. Horses that willingly carry their owner fearlessly over obstacles when they perhaps can't see the landing site have to have incredible trust in their owner, because horses are not only very many times stronger than a man, and therefore can't be forced to do anything they really don't want to, they are also prey animals, given naturally to suspicion rather than trust.

Carol Walker's story demonstrates beautifully the sheer unselfishness of our animal companions. There is no vanity and no jealousy in their world. This horse cared deeply, not only for his owner, but also for his own brother.

My gorgeous Arabian gelding, Ramsay, had a very unusual temperament for an Arab horse. He was very beautiful, with the traditional 'carved' head that made him look as if he was made of porcelain. He was chestnut with a blond mane and tail, and had tremendous 'presence'. But to ride he was a real sweetheart, calm and responsive and balanced, whereas some Arabians can be a bit 'high energy' for the average rider. I never felt a moment's fear when I was on him, even in heavy traffic. He wasn't even spooked by juggernauts. Sadly, I believe it was his lack of respect for traffic that was his downfall.

One night someone opened the gate to the field he was in, along with nine other horses, and they all got out. We pieced together the events of the night later. It seemed that the horses all meandered along the quiet lane the field opened onto, grazing the lush grass that they normally couldn't reach from the other side of the fence. It was a warm summer evening and I imagine they were all relaxed. Gradually their grazing nibbles took them down the lane towards open countryside beyond. They should have all been safe, and they were – all except for Ramsay.

It seems that while the others continued walking and grazing, something gave Ramsey a fright and he started off along the footpath at the bottom of the lane, in the opposite direction taken by the other horses, which were found safe and well in the morning. Ramsay must have galloped along the footpath until he came to a junction, and then, wanting to find his way home, he turned up towards the main road that ran along to the top of the stable's lane, thinking, I imagine, that this was the quickest way home.

Poor Ramsay didn't stand a chance. He ran straight out into the road right in front of a speeding lorry. Another horse might have backed off when he heard the huge vehicle coming, but Ramsay wasn't afraid of them at all.

I was totally devastated when I was woken by the police coming to tell me what had happened. I went into total shock, and the rest of what happened was, mercifully, a bit of a blur. Ramsay had already been removed by the time I reached the scene, but of course the lorry that killed him was still there. I felt sorry for the driver. It hadn't been his fault. One of my main concerns was to speak to the attending vet and make sure that Ramsay had been killed outright. Having not been there I was worried that he might have been in pain, with me not there for him. The vet assured me that the catastrophic injuries had killed my horse instantly.

The next few weeks went by in a daze of anguish. I'd lost my rock, and I wasn't sure I'd be able to continue riding, which I loved, without him. I knew for sure that I'd never have another horse like Ramsay. I tried, though. The hole left in my life was so big, I had to try and fill it somehow, because I really didn't want to give up. But luck wasn't on my side. I tried three horses over the next six months, and every one had to be returned as they were all totally unsuitable for me.

Then I thought I might have found the answer. It turned out that Ramsay had a full brother, and he was for sale.

When I first saw him I couldn't breathe, because he was the exact double of my horse. There were differences, though, because this horse was skinny and his mane and tail were matted. His eyes were runny and his feet were long and untrimmed. He had a pot belly and was obviously riddled with worms. He wasn't as unflappable as Ramsay had been, either, but that was just down to training. When I rode him I felt confident that this horse could be the answer to my prayers. But I still couldn't commit to him. I think part of me worried that Ramsay might feel betrayed, that seeing another horse identical to him in the field would make it all feel wrong. I didn't want another disappointment. I went back to the yard, deep in thought, to be met by a friend, Jane, who said the weirdest thing to me. 'So, you found one then? He's totally gorgeous!'

'What?' I asked, totally dumbfounded.

'A Ramsay lookalike. It's nice seeing that beautiful type of horse again.'

It turned out that she'd just come back from getting her own horse in and had seen a new horse that looked exactly like Ramsay, cantering and generally showing off, up and down the bottom side of the field.

She saw the stunned and perplexed look on my face and we both rushed out to see this 'new' horse. There was nothing there. Three times we walked the field, counting and identifying all the horses, thinking we'd gone mad.

There was no new horse. It had to have been Ramsay, telling me that he was happy with my choice, and that a horse like him did belong in that field. I bought the horse and called him Murad, which means 'wanted'. He's turned into a dream horse just like his brother, and he's now healthy and glossy and much loved. I can't believe I've been so lucky again.

Ramsay's brother had obviously fallen into bad hands. Carol told me that as well as being neglected, he'd had whip marks on his skinny flanks. She'd felt that his days would be numbered if he was left where she found him. Could it be that Ramsay had even died to save his brother? Carol wasn't 'lucky' with finding this horse, she was obviously appreciated as a wonderful owner by Ramsay and he wanted his brother to share in his 'luck' too, so Carol was led to find Murad. There are no such things as coincidences!

That story and the next one are very similar to ones I experienced myself with a much-loved pony called Baloo, who died after being hit by a car. It seems that horses have their own special ways of coming back to see us.

This is a Canadian story, from Corrine Bailey. Like her pony, my Baloo was a scrawny, scruffy, skinny boy, who turned into royalty under lavish attention.

I called my pony Jasper because his colouring was very like that precious stone. His coat was a rich red, and it wasn't until he was well into his twenties that the colour started to fade and turn grey. I bought him at an auction. Everyone else ignored him apart from the dealers who wanted a bargain, because he was dusty, ragged-looking and stood stubbornly with his ears back when the men tried to get him to run around the pen. If any of them came too close, armed with a stick or not, Jasper would bare his teeth and run away, and then turn with a nifty twist at the last second and ping his back feet towards them. He never actually kicked or bit anyone, though. He was skinny and his back legs bowed together at the hocks. So why did I buy him? It wasn't because I felt sorry for him, although I did. It was something in his eyes, some sort of spark that meant his spirit was still in there, underneath that musty coat.

Of course I had a bit of trouble loading him onto my trailer, and had to be a bit nippy myself, dodging those teeth and feet, but I was canny. I had my elderly pony Smokey in the trailer, and when Jasper saw him he turned sweet enough and walked right in. When I got him home I turned him out in the paddock with Smokey and just left him for a few days to unwind. Then I took Smokey away (he would come to my call) and I went into the field with a bucket of feed, thinking Jasper (as I'd already named him) would be a pussycat for food. I was wrong! When I got to within 20 feet of him he came at me backwards, feet flying! I skipped smartly to one side and then whump, whacked him on the behind with the bucket. It wasn't done to hurt him. The bucket was only plastic. It was more the noise I wanted, just to shake him up a bit and let him know that I was the boss, not him!

That pony was incredibly intelligent. Right away he knuckled under, coming to me and looking very chastened. I found out later he'd been cared for by unattended children and had quickly learned to intimidate them to avoid their attentions, which was why he was so skinny and so scruffy. From that day on we never had a cross word. I'm lucky that I'm small, which means I can ride ponies rather than bigger horses. I prefer ponies because they are generally smarter, and Jasper was the best. His coat soon had a beautiful shine, a combination of good grooming and the right food. That was when I added the word 'King' to his name, and King Jasper was born.

Jasper really loved his hay, pretty much more than grass, which is unusual in a pony.

I had him 32 years, which made him about 38 when he passed away; a good age. One morning I found him just lying in the field, stone dead. He'd passed in the night. My only regret was that I'd never said goodbye, although during those last few years I always knew when I hung his hay net each night that I might be saying goodbye when I left him. I kind of hoped that's the way it would go, because I sure didn't relish ever having to have him shot.

A few weeks later I was standing in the field shelter, right where Jasper used to stand, hanging a hay net for my new pony. He was a lovely creature, not as young as Jasper had been when I got him, because I was no spring chicken myself by then. The pony was still in the stall at this point because I wanted to hang the hay net before I let him out. He was a bit fretful and I thought the food being there would settle him, rather than have him go chasing round the field in the near dark. I hung the net and stood back. Jasper was on my mind and I could almost see him waiting for me to step back so that he could get to his hay.

That was when the hay net started to move. There was no wind and I watched, transfixed, wondering what on earth was making it sway. Then I realized what was happening. The net had taken on a characteristic movement – characteristic, that is, of when a live horse eats the hay. The net would sway gently, then stop, move sharply the other way (as if a horse were tugging at a mouthful of the hay), then commence swinging freely again, only to be stopped and snatched again. There was no doubt in my mind that Jasper was there, eating that hay just as when he was alive. I chuckled to myself, *Don't they have hay in heaven, boy?* I watched that net for about five minutes, and then I came back to earth with a thump as the new pony started yelling his head off for me to let him out. I glanced away, glanced back, and apart from a little residual movement, the hay net hung still. To this day I have never forgotten that Jasper came back to see me. It's given me a whole new perspective on life.

Baloo, my old pony, did a very similar thing with me after he'd died, snatching at a hanging hay net while I was musing on whether my new horse was the right one for me. Previously he'd been seen and heard galloping in the field, twice. In his case it was as if by galloping frantically he'd been telling me the two other horses I'd looked at had been wrong, but by peacefully munching his hay he signalled his approval of the new boy.

Chapter 3

Guardian Pets

'Histories are more full of examples of the fidelity of dogs
than of friends.'
— Alexander Pope

It's a really beautiful thought that pets who have protected and watched over us while they're alive might continue to do so after we've lost them. I felt very privileged to have the following selection of stories sent to me, because they not only reinforce my belief that our pets have souls, but also prove that death isn't the end, either for them or for us.

Sharon Brooker's story about Tara is heartwarming.

The 12 months between 1996 and 1997 were the toughest of my life. This was the time when I lost not only my nan, whom I loved dearly, but also my precious dog, Tara. Then I got sick, too. My nan, who was my mum's mum, was called Doreen Page. She was a beautiful, statuesque lady, with pure white hair. She was six feet tall, very graceful, and everyone said that she was a 'real lady'. She owned a racehorse once, and ran her own steel business until she left the UK to live in Spain. As youngsters, my sister and I used to stay some weekends with her in her apartment down by the seafront, on Canvey Island in Essex. When she moved to Spain I used to fly out there for school holidays. My most abiding memory of her is her wonderful infectious laugh. In 1996 Nan was diagnosed with terminal cancer, and we had just one short month to say goodbye to her. My dog Tara was a cross-breed. As a puppy she had been one of the ugliest of the litter, which just made her all the more beautiful to me. She was about the size of a springer spaniel. She had a short, glossy coat, and a long tail with a white tuft on the end. Her main colour was black, with four tan-and-white legs, a tan-and-white chest, and her face was black and tan with a fox-like white nose and beautiful dark brown eyes. She always literally used to smile when her photo was taken. She sometimes used to sleep curved round my head on my pillow, and I'd sleep with her nose poking in my ear. Tara was the best kind of dog. She was faithful and gentle, and we adored each other. She would lie on the settee with me, pouring her long body into the space between me and the back of the settee. She'd rest her head on my shoulder and I'd feel her wet nose pressed against my neck. I'd feel so safe and secure with her. One of her less endearing habits, but just another reason I loved her, was that she would chew her marrowbone for a while and then take it out into the garden and bury it. She'd reappear, paws and muzzle all covered with mud, a big grin plastered on her face. The really yucky bit came later, when she'd go and find the bone again, often months later, when it was all slimy and covered in mould, and drag it all over the lounge carpet, leaving a trail of mud and unidentifiable gunge behind her. If she wasn't spotted and stopped, she'd then take it upstairs and place it tenderly on the floor next to my bed for me to find later. Tara got sick that year, too. I looked after her night and day; nothing was too much trouble. She had to have radiotherapy, but it was unsuccessful at shrinking her brain tumour. Finally, and this I think was what made me ill, I had to make the hardest decision of my life and put Tara out of her misery. That was in June 1997. My health got worse and I discovered I had ME. This is an awful illness, and the worst of it is that some people won't even accept that you're ill. I suffered constant tiredness and aching joints. Sometimes it was so bad I couldn't face getting out of bed unless I could fall straight into a hot bath. I got more and more depressed and barely had the energy to walk my other dogs. It was only Tara I wanted. Then one day after a walk I came back to find big, muddy blobs dotted right across the lounge carpet. I couldn't believe it. They certainly hadn't been there when I went out. I followed the dirt trail upstairs, already sure of what

I would find. Sure enough, there beside my bed was a big, muddy bone, blue with mould. I was sure it was Tara who'd put it there. None of my other dogs ever buried their bones, and they certainly didn't dig them up again and put them by my bed. That was Tara's trick, and anyway the dogs had been out with me. A few days later I got confirmation that it had been Tara. I was in the bedroom and, out of the corner of my eye, I saw the tuft of a tail, her tail, just disappearing round the door. I ran out to look but there was nothing there.

My ME became more and more debilitating and miserable. I started to really think I couldn't take any more. I lay on my bed and all I wanted to do was go to sleep and never wake up. But I had a dream, and the dream saved me, or Tara did. I dreamed I was in a grassy meadow. I could see all the colours so vividly, the rich green grass and the white picket fence that surrounded the meadow. There was a little path across the grass and it led down to a gate and out onto the hills beyond. My nan was there, standing right by the gate. And Tara was just a few feet away from me, the most natural place for her to be. She wagged her tail furiously and ran to me. I couldn't believe how wonderful she looked, so healthy, and I felt healthy at that moment too. I looked at my nan and she waved at me, smiling. I hugged Tara and she licked my face, licked the tears of joy that were running down my cheeks. I could hardly speak, but I told her that I had missed her so much, and I said, 'Mummy loves you Tara, Mummy loves you so much.' It was wonderful. After a while, though, Tara started to walk away. She went a few steps and then looked over her shoulder at me. I didn't want her to go. I could hardly bear it. I begged her not to go, and after she kept walking further away, and turning to look, I started to hurry after her. But I could hear my nan speaking. She was saying, 'No, Sharon, you can't come.' I understood. If I followed them, it really would be the end of my life, and I'd never be waking up back on my bed. Tara reached my nan, and Nan bent down to stroke Tara. Nan looked up and smiled at me, and Tara turned and wagged her tail one last time, then the two of them went through the gate and gradually disappeared from sight. Next minute I was awake in my bed. I felt alone, but I also knew somehow that my life wasn't over after all, and that I'd get on with it again. My nan and Tara came back to save me, to tell me that I still had a life and that I could beat the ME. I *will* do it, for them, because they saved my life that day.

This next story came from Jane Tarbuck. I'd heard about dogs being trained to sense illness, and I'd heard about dogs coming back to save their owners from danger, but this story encompasses both these things.

My poodle Roxie was the light of my life. From the day we picked her up as a sweet, chocolate ball of fluff, I lived in dread of the inevitable day when she'd leave me. We all know that, don't we, even if we don't talk about it, that our beloved pets will leave us one day? Roxie was a toy poodle, so she was tiny, not exactly guard dog material, but that didn't matter to her. She was ultra-protective of me, fussing and worrying over me if I was upset or ill, and staunchly defending me against any perceived threat. I suppose I was one of the lucky ones, because at 16 years of age Roxie just didn't wake up one day. When I woke up, there was her little body curled on the bottom of the bed, where she'd always slept. I waited expectantly for her to spring to her feet and come to give me a kiss, as usual, but she didn't move. My heart clamped up in my chest as I realized that Roxie was no more. Life would never be the same again. The house was as empty as my life, and I grieved as much as anyone would for a child or a husband. That's how much difference she'd made in my life.

I never thought I'd see her again.

I'd always had poor eyesight and had to make sure I took regular check-ups at the optician's to be able to keep seeing anything at all, but after Roxie died I just couldn't be bothered. I got to the point where I knew my eyesight was deteriorating but didn't do anything about it. My eyes became red and sore. Then one evening I was flicking through TV channels, watching an ever-more-blurry and ever-more-boring succession of images. I hadn't even bothered to put my specs on because I wasn't really interested in anything the television had to offer. They were lying on the floor next to the beanbag I was sitting on. Suddenly something caught my attention, a dark shadow that seemed to be emerging from the wall. I instinctively reached for my glasses, but as my hand brushed them the 'shadow' leapt across the room and pounced on them. The shadow materialized as it leapt, into a small brown poodle. While I gasped in astonishment, the poodle, my Roxie, grabbed at the glasses. Her mouth passed right through them, and she pounced again, and then I heard her excited little yap, the one she always did when she was desperately trying to make me understand something, then she vanished.

I was totally ecstatic that Roxie was obviously still around and not entirely lost to me, and tears filled my eyes. The salty tears reminded me how sore my eyes had been getting of late, as they stung, and that's when I understood what Roxie was trying to tell me. She wanted me to get my eyes checked. I went to the optician's the next day, to discover that I was developing glaucoma. The optician said he didn't know what had made me come after missing so many appointments, but whatever it was had saved my sight, because without treatment I would certainly have gone blind. Roxie always was my guardian ... and she still is.

Jeff Gordon contacted me from the USA to tell me the story of his horse, Chester. Jeff was so proud of him that when he talked to me on the phone about Chester's accomplishments I could hear the emotion in his voice. I can't blame him, because Chester does indeed sound very special.

My horse was *the* horse, the best one that ever lived. He was really smart and I taught him all kinds of tricks. He could count, tell colours apart, shake hands, bow, almost anything a dog could do. He could even 'fetch' things. He played ball with a giant one, rolling it around with his feet. He lived until he was 25 years old. Of course I'd had him since he was a foal and we were really close. Chester trusted me and I trusted him. He was a Quarter Horse, which is the best kind in my opinion, and he was the reddest mahogany bay you ever saw. We had a wonderful time together all through his life, and I don't believe I ever once said a cross word to him.

When he had to be put down after breaking a leg I was devastated. He was a good age, but he could have lived until he was 40 or more. I vowed never to have another horse. Chester was a one-off and I didn't want another. We didn't have any other horses on the property so that kind of beauty vanished from our lives.

Then something very strange happened. Last year it was (2007). I was in bed asleep when I got woken up by a horse whinnying. You know how it is when you get woken up by a noise – for a while you're not sure what it is. Then my wife Jenny said, 'What was that noise? It sounded like … well, it sounded like Chester.'

Of course it couldn't be, but she was right, when it came again it did sound like Chester. You might think one horse would sound just like another, but they have their different voices, same as us. The horse was doing Chester's 'Hurry up' voice. It was shrill, impatient, and maybe a little scared. It was coming from right under our bedroom window. I jumped out of bed and looked out the window. There was no horse. What terrified me more at the time than an invisible horse was the smoke coming from the barn. It was on fire!

We were lucky we weren't too far out of town and the fire was under control pretty quickly. It had been caused by an electrical fault. Once we were all calmed down and the insurance forms filled in, we had time to think. Jenny and I both believe that Chester came back to save us. Fire is something that all horses fear, and that might have been enough to bring him back. He saved us both, and the house. The way the wind was blowing, the whole place would have gone up if we hadn't woken up. I'm thinking now, maybe he wouldn't mind if I got another foal, especially if I called it Little Chester.

It seems that all animals have the capacity to come back to their owner after death when a dangerous situation arrives. It was the same for Carrie Chestnut and her cat, Lucky.

We called our cat Lucky because we figured she was very fortunate we came along when we did, as she was the last of an unwanted litter of barn cats and was about to meet her maker courtesy of a bucket of water. It turned out *we* were the lucky ones.

We lived in a nice cottage-style house, which was a bit shabby but big enough for us and comfortable. Lucky grew up there, and she was a great cat. Jet black with a tiny white star on her nose, she was very pretty, and we'd been shocked that her owner was going to kill her without giving her much of a chance in life. Anyway, she was really well behaved and she never wasted her time bringing us useless things like dead mice, or even rats. Oh no, Lucky would go out across the fields and bring us rabbits, something we could eat and something that would supplement the family's food budget. It might seem mean, but I'd rather eat a wild rabbit than a pig that's known nothing but a tiny pen all its life.

When she got ill 14 years later we were very upset. Lucky had a stroke and went totally blind. We tried so hard to keep her going, but it was terrible. She was never an indoors cat, and if you kept her in she would just cry and yowl to be let out. She was just miserable. If we let her out she'd be all right for a while and then she'd lose her bearings and we'd find her sitting out in the middle of the lane, a sitting target for any fast car that came along. Even a slow car could have easily hit her because she wouldn't see it coming or know which way to run.

It took me a while, but in the end I decided that she was trying to tell me she wanted to go. I won't go as far as saying she wanted to kill herself and that when she sat in the road she knew exactly what she was doing, but it seemed that way sometimes.

I finally did the deed, holding her in my arms while the injection from the vet took effect and Lucky went limp. We buried her out in the woods, nice and deep so nothing would dig her up, and built a little stone cairn over her.

It was sad without her. I'd keep seeing her shape flitting around in the corner of my eye, but when I turned there was never anything to be seen. I never got another cat.

We'd got older, the children left home and then it was just me and my husband Jeff. The house had got older, too, and we never did seem to have enough money to fix anything. A few weeks before the event I'm going to tell you about, during the dead of winter, I started to feel ill. I had a lot of headaches and I felt hung-over all the time, but we rarely drank anything alcoholic because we rarely had the cash, so it wasn't that. I thought it was some kind of flu. Jeff didn't get so badly affected because, as we figured later, he wasn't in the house as much as me.

One night I'd gone to bed early because I felt so rough, and it wasn't long before I was in a really deep sleep. Something woke me up at about 3 a.m. I knew something was wrong because Jeff wasn't beside me, but I didn't seem to care. I couldn't get up. Then I heard a plaintive *meow* and it sounded just like Lucky. *Oh*, I thought, *you know where it's warm, don't you, puss?* I reached out with my hand, sleepily, and my fingers found her soft fur. I snuggled up to her. Part of me was thinking, *Hang on, she's dead, Lucky's dead,* but the rest of me just wanted to sleep, no matter what.

As I said, Lucky was a good cat, and she never ever scratched or bit anyone. So when I felt her fangs digging into my fingers, piercing the skin, I fairly leapt out of bed, grabbing at my hand to stem the blood. I was dizzy, and I flicked on the light. There was no cat. There was no blood. I turned my hand over and over, thinking it must have been some dream! Then I realized how dizzy and sick I actually felt, and that Jeff hadn't come to bed. I staggered downstairs, barely keeping my feet, to find him out cold on the sofa. The gas boiler was roaring away, and suddenly it hit me. Carbon monoxide poisoning! I grabbed Jeff and shook him. When that didn't work I slapped him as hard as I could.

That worked and we both staggered out into the frosty air. The fresh air in our lungs soon revived us, and I was able to go to a neighbour's and phone for an ambulance. Like I said at the beginning, *we* were the lucky ones.

Merle was a farm dog who took her duties really seriously. Collies like this often regard the whole family as their responsibility, and will herd them just like sheep or cattle if it's for their own good. Kristy Willis sent me this story of a dog whose sense of duty never died.

We were aged 12 and 15, me and my brother Danny, when we went for a week's holiday with our auntie in Dorset. It wasn't much of a holiday, to be honest, as it was on a farm and we already lived on a farm at home in Wiltshire. I think Mum sent us there just to get us out of her hair, really, rather than for our sake. The six-week school holidays must have seemed like years to her. Anyway, it was a nice week, and we enjoyed the different countryside, but we were both bored and itching to get back to our computers at home.

If it had just been down to me I don't think anything weird would've happened, because I would've gone home the conventional route, no matter how long it took, not being keen on trudging round the wet countryside in the dark. What happened was that by the time we got all the connecting trains and ended up at our home station, it was almost dark, being about 9.30 p.m. There'd been a delay and we'd missed our bus, the one that passed right by the end of our driveway. There'd be another one, but we'd have to wait a whole hour.

Danny reckoned we could walk the rest of the way in about half that time. I didn't want to because I thought it would take twice that. No, he said, not if we go 'as the crow flies'. We could, he insisted, walk cross-country, using footpaths and tracks and fields, and cut the time in half. It sounded logical so I reluctantly agreed. I don't think either one of us took any notice of the fact that it was clouding over, so the stars and moon wouldn't be out to guide our way once it was full dark. We set off, both tucking our jeans into our socks to avoid getting them all wet in the long grass.

It was perfectly fine at first, and we made good time, but that was because we were on stone footpaths and mown fields. Once it was really dark I realized how silly we'd been, because we couldn't see more than a few feet ahead. People who live in towns have no idea how dark the countryside can be once you move away from all street lighting. We didn't get lost, exactly, because now and again we saw the twinkling lights of a cottage or farmhouse that we could identify. I was just about ready to go and knock on a door by then, though, because my legs were soaked despite my precautions, and I was sick of having brambles and other branches whip suddenly across my face out of the dark, but just in time Danny said, 'Here we are, in the back meadow, we're almost home.' Immediately, thoughts of a hot shower and a pleasant hour of checking and answering my emails cheered me up and I pressed on, happily. We both knew that we just had to cross the railway sleeper bridge from this meadow to the next, and then we could walk across the last field and we'd be in the yard.

We stumbled along, feeling for the gap that would signal the end of the bridge. Just at that moment we both nearly had a heart attack as Dad's collie, Merle, appeared out of the darkness. Merle could be a bit of a pain and she thought she was meant to herd *everything,* including us, but we were pleased to see her as it confirmed that we were home.

Danny let out a whoop when his searching fingers found the gate on our side of the bridge and he started fiddling with the latch, moaning because the gate was usually open while the field was empty, and he knew that the cattle weren't in that field yet. They never went in there until late August and this was only mid July. Finally he managed to flip the bolt, but before he could actually swing the gate open, it all went wrong because Merle wouldn't let us cross the bridge. She kept barking and bouncing in our way, and when that didn't work she actually growled at us, showing her teeth. I'd always been a bit wary of her, so I told Danny that we should give up and go the long way round. Reluctantly, he agreed. Even his bravado had taken a walk by then, so we backtracked to the hedge and climbed the gate that led into the lane. By following the lane for a few hundred yards we came to the end of the drive and could walk from there easily, even if it added about ten minutes to the journey.

Merle had vanished, thank goodness, and we made our way home with no further adventures. When we got in, Mum first of all exclaimed and complained over our scratches, and the mud that plastered our trainers and jeans, and then told us she had some sad news. She said that Merle had run down the lane and been killed by a lorry. We were shocked, upset, but also totally amazed. How could Merle have been dead when we'd just seen her? Mum's face turned white as we told her what had happened, not least because for once Dad had put the cows and calves in the field Merle had stopped us going through. Cows can be very dangerous if they think their babies are being threatened, and two kids feeling their way through a dark field would certainly have aroused their aggressive protective instincts. In the dark, if they'd tried to trample us, we'd have been helpless.

There are many stories out there about a huge white dog that's appeared in various locations and saved people from danger. It's not the spirit of anyone's pet, and has no apparent connection with the people it saves. One woman was saved from being shot when the dog appeared and refused to let her enter a room where a fight was just breaking out. Another man was pushed, in front of witnesses, down some steps into a cellar, when seconds later shots rang out and a man was killed on the front lawn of the house. Where do these mystical guardians come from? Another time? Another space? Another dimension?

I was lucky enough to be sent this personal story about a strange dog by artist Nicola J T MacMillan. Her story only deepens the mystery, and was so astounding that I had to include it.

My grandfather on my father's side was a wonderful man, a gentle soul who'd be the first in line to help anybody. Because he was an excellent mechanic, my mother's father had roped him in and asked for help with the maintenance of his ice-cream van. My grandfather worked on the van all day and evening, and when he'd finished he climbed into the driver's seat and started up the engine. The ice-cream van ran smoothly, so he felt able to return it back to the depot so that my mother's father wouldn't lose another day's work. He dropped off the van and got a lift back to his works in order to collect his car. Finally, he was able to set off for home. It was a winter's night and black ice was hidden within the tarmac of the busy Liverpool roads. As he was approaching Hillfoot Avenue, my grandfather felt drawn to look to his right, in the direction of Allerton cemetery. Having family members buried there, he said a small prayer for them as he continued to drive home. Then, turning back to the dual carriageway, he saw that there was a man standing there thumbing a lift. The man had an animal, a dog, standing next to him. It was past midnight and grandfather knew it was freezing, so he stopped for the man and his dog. Pulling over to the side of the road, Grandfather wound down his window. He asked the hitchhiker where he wanted to go. Within a blink of an eye, the man disappeared. The hairs on the back of my grandfather's neck stood on end, and he felt an almighty chill go through his body. At the same time, the dog leaped up through the open window and sat on the passenger seat, giving my grandfather another fright because he hadn't realized that the dog was still there! Quickly winding the window back up, my grandfather drove away, feeling very nervous and shaky.

His mind raced with wonder as to where the man had gone, and whether he was a spirit who'd appeared to make sure his dog was safe. In any case the dog was quite real and couldn't be abandoned in the icy weather. When they got home, the dog followed my grandfather into the house, where they were greeted by my nan and great-grandmother. My dad, who at that time was a young teenager, was tucked up in bed fast asleep. While grandfather was still puzzling over the weird events of the night, he fed his new pet and made him a bed for the night.

The following day it was decided that the dog could stay, and they named him Kim, as his collar had the initial 'K' engraved onto it. He was a black-and-white Alsatian, lovely and soft-natured, with a shiny coat and healthy physique. Kim soon became a member of the family. He was an excellent guard dog and he'd stay with Grandfather throughout the day at his garage. Kim was also great company and Grandfather was thrilled to have him by his side. A full year passed, and then on the anniversary of the mysterious day that my grandfather had found Kim, he lost him. The day seemed like an ordinary one, and my grandfather went to work with Kim. Finishing early, he decided to take the rest of the afternoon off, and so he quickly packed up and headed home. After parking his car, he stepped out with Kim, his shadow, right behind him. The chimes from a local ice-cream van rang out, and Grandfather turned to cross the road and buy his children an ice cream before going indoors. After he was served he walked, with his neighbour, to the back of the van and started to cross the road. Milliseconds later a car carrying a gang of youths went speeding past the ice-cream van and were about to plough into my grandfather. Kim saw the danger and jumped into him, pushing him and the neighbour backwards. Poor Kim was hit by the car and killed instantly.

Distraught at his loss, Grandfather couldn't believe the bravery of his beloved pet. Kim was cremated, and Grandfather chose to bury him with his family in Allerton cemetery, right opposite the place where they'd first met.

Two months later, while he was driving down Hillfoot Avenue, Grandfather spotted the same hitchhiker he'd seen there before, and sure enough his dog was standing beside him. Stunned, Grandfather pulled over, and watched in disbelief as the man vanished before his eyes again, only this time Kim disappeared, too. Had Kim been sent to save my grandfather's life, and had the connection of my mother's father's ice-cream van united them? Or had he simply returned to his previous owner after having been looked after for a year? Many still report seeing the hitchhiker and his pet, and we wonder, will Kim return one day to save another life?

Chapter 4

Pets That Return

'I died as a mineral and became a plant,
I died as a plant and rose to animal,
I died as animal and I was man.
Why should I fear?
When was I less by dying?'
– JALALU 'D-DIN RUMI, SUFI POET

We never get ultimate proof when an animal returns to us in a new body, but maybe we're not meant to. Proof like that could change the world, and maybe not in a good way. If everyone believed 100 per cent in reincarnation, quite a few people might give up on this life and hope for a better one next time, for instance.

These stories don't give us proof that pets have returned, but they have given comfort to their owners, and that's the great thing.

Janet Schofield sent me this sweet story about her little dog.

Russ is a short-haired miniature Jack Russell. He was actually given to my mum and dad by my niece as a 'therapy dog' for my mum, who wasn't well at the time, and still isn't. He arrived in December 2000 and we always celebrate his birthday on the 7th of November, with a cupcake with a candle in. Nowadays, when we have a birthday for him and we sing happy birthday, he starts to sing with us. Mum and Dad think this is great. I've also taught Russ to say hello, and it almost does sound like he is saying just that. He's seven now and he sleeps with Mum and Dad on their bed.

Russ seems almost human at times. He has to sit at the dinner table with us, and eats his dog biscuits there while we have our breakfast. He has a sweet tooth and he likes to start the day with something sugary, and he loves to lick Mum's cereal bowl (after she's finished with it, of course). He insists also on licking the dessert bowls, because like I said he has a very sweet tooth. Most of the time he's an all-round family dog, but he gets a bit weird when he's given his main meal at night. He won't eat it unless I'm sitting in the lounge with him. I have to play with him to get him to eat it. The reason that's so weird is that, to be honest, I don't really like dogs much. He wasn't bought for me and I just can't understand why he acts that way.

This might sound really silly, but I've been thinking that Russ is someone I've known before, someone who's been reincarnated as a dog. This is because his eating habits remind me of my grandfather, as he liked to eat his dessert first and then his main meal, and the way he fusses around all of us, especially if someone is sick. He does this more if it's me, and sometimes it just feels like my grandfather is back.

This story from Sarah Brenner gives much more convincing evidence for a dog returning in a new body. It totally amazed me when I first read it, so I hope it amazes you, too.

When I looked at the puppy in the basket, she looked more like a drowned rat than a dog. She'd just been bathed by the rescue centre staff, and although she'd been more or less dried, her very short coat was lying so tight and damp to her skin that it virtually wasn't there at all. Her grey colour didn't help dispel the likeness to a rodent. She was a chihuahua crossed with something unknown, and my hubby, Ray, always said perhaps she was crossed with a rat, which I thought was a little unkind! She wasn't the prettiest dog in the world, having a slightly overshot top jaw which made her teeth look a little goofy. It didn't matter to me. I picked her up, looked into her big brown eyes and it was love at first sight. From that moment she owned me. Ray loved her too, even though he tried not to show it. The day I bought her home, all skinny and nearly hairless, she found a place in his heart.

I called her Teacup. A silly name, but it suited her because she was as dainty as bone china. She didn't have a china nature, though. She was mischievous and bright and when she wanted me to pick her up she was a tyrant, screeching and wailing as if she was being attacked by a giant Rottweiler! It was naughty, really, but I loved the attention she gave me. She'd embarrass Ray if he was waiting with her outside shops while I was inside doing the shopping. Pirouetting around on her hind legs and crying, she'd make an exhibition of herself.

She had a total passion for custard cream biscuits, and would be really bad over them. It was her worst and naughtiest fault. You couldn't trust her at all if you had one; she'd use every trick in the book to get it from you, even sneaking up the back of the chair and whipping it out of your unsuspecting hand with all the skill of a marauding seagull! Such a tiny dog, she barely grew much bigger than she was as a pup, but she had the heart the size of a lion's.

She lived a long time and I was very glad of that. There was a while when I thought she'd live for ever, but of course she didn't. There came that dreaded day all dog owners have to face. I was very lucky, though, as apart from having to have her sticky-out teeth cleaned a couple of times a year, she hadn't had to see the vet at all during her lifetime. The night she died was just like any other. She went out to do her toilet, went to her bed, snuggled up with the fur-covered hot-water bottle we'd never been able to wean her off, and I told her, 'Goodnight, sweetheart,' as always, and went to bed.

The next morning when I came down, I knew immediately because never would she have stayed in her bed when I was up. She looked so peaceful, still curled round her bottle even though it was cold now. I picked her up, and I could tell by her slight stiffness that she'd been gone for hours, probably soon after I'd left her. I cried and cried, and Ray came down to see what was wrong, and he cried too.

The next few months were full of hurt, coming home and forgetting as I turned the key, only to be reminded by the silence and stillness. Ray kept asking if we should find another one to rescue, but my heart still belonged to Teacup. I honestly thought it always would. Then a couple of years later something completely miraculous happened while Ray and I were on holiday, in a cottage in the Lake District. It was somewhere we'd been many times before. We loved the area and knew it very well. Our cottage was remote, so remote that Ray said that, as we were getting on a bit, we should think about looking for somewhere less cut off, but I loved it there.

One morning I was making a brew. Ray wandered into the kitchen, answering the call of the smell of frying bacon. I heard a scratch at the door.

'What's that?' I asked.

'I don't know,' answered Ray, settling in front of his plate. I took the hint and went and opened the top of the stable door myself. There was no one there. Then I heard a whine and looked down. There stood the prettiest dog I've ever seen. It was a little fluff-ball with the most gorgeous black coat. It was gazing up at me with the biggest brown eyes through a Beatle-style fringe. I looked down and the dog looked up.

'Who are you?' I asked.

'Who're you talking to?' asked Ray.

'It's a little dog,' I said, opening the bottom of the door.

The dog came in. Ray looked at it, smiled, and offered it a scrap of bacon. The dog, with no questions asked, jumped up onto the chair opposite him as if it had done it every day for years. We took the dog home at the end of the holiday, because no one claimed it, and we were so far from anywhere that she was surely a stray.

Penny, as we called her, was a member of the family within a day, but I felt a bit uneasy. I felt I'd betrayed Teacup. Ray said I was being silly. Then that evening I was sitting looking at her while Ray was making a cup of tea, and her face just changed. The black shaggy hair vanished and was suddenly grey and smooth. Her pretty face suddenly had buck teeth. I blinked. It was Teacup's face looking back at me. Then she sneezed. Her face juddered and she was back as Penny. I thought I was going bonkers and thought, *I won't mention that to Ray!* He came in from the kitchen at that point and handed me a cup of tea and two custard creams. Like a flash, like greased lightning, Penny launched herself from the chair next to me, latched her little teeth onto the custard cream and was gone behind the sofa with it before I could move.

'My God!' shouted Ray. 'That's weird!'

Not half as weird as what I saw, I thought. There was no doubt in my mind that Penny was Teacup. I had my baby back.

We sometimes come back in a very different form to what we had in a past life, in order to live a very different life, so it makes sense to me that Teacup would choose to come back so much prettier than she was before. She was so opposite to the way she looked before that it seems right, somehow, balanced. It seems that she didn't change her eating habits, though!

Holly Davis lives in Wales and is a horse communicator, so it didn't surprise me that she'd had an amazing experience of her own. So many people go through their lives waiting for that 'something missing' to arrive in their lives and change it. This is how it happened to Holly.

My interest in horses first began when my daughter, Charlotte, started riding lessons. Soon after that we were offered a beautiful Arab crossbred mare called Kayleigh, to buy. Knowing little about horses and so not being very cautious, and probably not very wise, I jumped right in and bought her, and she soon arrived home with us. We were quick to find out that she wasn't a novice ride, and yet within three months I was riding her out on the road in her head collar. It was just as if, for no real reason, we'd just trusted each other right from the start. I found I could calm her just by thinking soft thoughts to her.

After we'd had her around three months, Kayleigh fell desperately ill one night, and she was diagnosed with surgical colic. It appeared that a tumour had wrapped around her intestines and had strangled them, and she was quite literally dying.

The next few weeks were a roller-coaster ride as Kayleigh went through not just one but two operations to save her life. The second operation was very drastic but it was her only hope for survival. All the time the operation was taking place I found myself listening to the John Denver song *Annie's Song*, or as I later renamed it, *Kayleigh's Song*, because whenever I hear it I always think of her. Kayleigh came home from hospital and slowly recovered, though it took many months. She was only around 13 years old and yet by this time it was becoming obvious that she also had a dreaded disease called Cushing's syndrome, which is a metabolic disorder.

Still, life was good for a while, but over time it became obvious that Kayleigh had a lot of bad things going on in her body for a horse of such a young age. During this time Kayleigh passed a message to me through a friend, telling her, 'I'm going to push you to your emotional limits. Stick with it, because this is for you and your beliefs. My body is not my own. It's a test.' I was panic-stricken by this message, but over time I pushed it to the back of my mind to a place where it was almost forgotten.

After this time Kayleigh continued to go downhill, including suffering chronic laminitis in her hooves, which made them painful. But Kayleigh, who'd always been able to send me telepathic messages, kept on telling me, 'You know how to make me better, you know how to make me well, and I will die of old age.' So I continued to do everything I could for her to make her comfortable. On reflection, if I'm honest, I can see now that to a degree I refused to see just how ill she was, as I couldn't bear the thought of losing her, not *my* mare.

I clearly recall the day I walked into the field and Kayleigh broadcast straight into my mind the words that I'd dreaded hearing. She was ready to go. I burst into tears, ran indoors and cried on my bed like a baby. Still she spoke in my mind, in a loving but firm way, basically telling me to pull myself together and to go back outside, which I did. She then showed me in my mind's eye an energy cord that ran from my stomach to her. She explained that I'd been feeding her energy in order to help keep her alive, and it had to stop. In the vision, the end that was attached to me was red and swollen, and sure enough I'd been suffering from stomach problems for many months. She told me that now was time to cut the cord and let her go. But, she told me, in order to do this I first had to love her 100 per cent – that the 97 per cent I now felt wasn't good enough! I can honestly say that it took me only minutes to feel the 100 per cent love as I cut the cord to let her go.

I stood in the field and looked at her, and for the first time I actually *saw* the reality of her. I almost gasped at the realization I'd been refusing to accept for months. At only 15 this mare was dying of old age. The poor girl looked about 30. Kayleigh explained to me that we both needed a few days to get used to the idea of her passing. She said that during this time we needed to spend time talking to each other and coming to terms with her passing. That was a Saturday, and she told me that Thursday would be a good day for her to go, so I booked the vet for her. The following day I had booked a stand at a local horse event and I didn't want to go and leave her, but she told me I was still to go as I needed to look out for a little yellow dog that had a message for me.

So the next day I dutifully set off on my travels, not really wanting to leave her at home, as the time we had left together was to be so short. On the way I decided to pull off at the motorway services for breakfast. As I sat eating my food I did something I'd never done before. I picked up the receipt that I had been given at the till and read it right through. At the bottom of the piece of paper I read the words, 'You have been served by Kayleigh.' As I read the words a cold shiver of realization ran down my spine. Yes, I had indeed been served by this mare. I tucked the piece of paper safely in my pocket, got back in my car and made my way to the event. As soon as I got out of the car I was greeted by the little yellow dog, who belonged to a vet who was there. I asked the dog if it had a message for me, and quickly heard her clear reply, 'It's been a pleasure to serve you!' At hearing this I couldn't help but laugh, because it seemed there were no limits to what this mare was going to do to make me feel at ease and know that she was around me, helping me. I spent the day happily working with people and their horse-related problems, and then made the long journey home.

The next few days, I'm glad to say, went slowly and I felt as if something had changed in me. Something had become peaceful. When the vet turned up on the Thursday morning I felt calm and happy in a strange sort of way. Kayleigh was first injected with a sedative followed by a lethal injection. I just stood and watched as she gently slipped to the ground. Somehow I could no long identify with the old worn-out body that lay on the ground at my feet, because this old used-up shell was no longer my mare. Little did my vet know at the time but I had been silently talking with Kayleigh throughout the whole event, and can honestly say that never once was there any break or distress in the conversation. It had been as if she had been stood there talking to me all of the time.

I thought this was the end of it until later that evening when I received a telephone call from a friend. She told me she had just been on an internet forum that we are both members of. There had been a new thread put on there only that day entitled, 'I don't know where this is from or who it's for,' and my friend felt I needed to go and read it, so I did. The message read …

> *'We are but one, I have not left,*
> *I stand by your side and guide you.*
> *Your dream is my dream and I will defend it to the last.*
> *We will walk together side by side,*
> *As you are my trusted friend and I your guide,*
> *Stepping silently in the sand.'*

'Is this you, Kay?' I asked. 'Yes,' she answered in my mind. 'Did you get the bit about stepping silently in the sand? It's from your favourite poem, "Footprints".' I had to laugh, as I emailed the lady, named Jay, who'd put up the post. She emailed back and asked me if 'sweets' meant anything to me, as in candy. Before the vet had arrived I'd given Kay two packets of Polo mints, something I hadn't given her in years.

That night as I walked down my driveway to lock the gate I heard Kayleigh's voice loud and clear. 'Look up,' she called, and as I did I saw the most beautiful shooting star. 'That's me,' she said softly. 'Each soul has a star.'

Rather than being the end of our story I feel that it is only just beginning. You see, Kay has never really left me. Just days after her death, while I was standing in the field, I heard her ask me for a cuddle. I turned around and I saw Anam Cara, my other beautiful Arab, looking me straight in the eye. It was her voice coming from him, and I instinctively threw my arms around him. It seems that Kay never really left completely. She chose to physically leave her body, but her wisdom, knowledge and, undoubtedly, her love, live on in the form of this beautiful boy, so that we could fulfil our journey and live out our shared dream together. Anam Cara totally changed that day, picking up all of Kay's mannerisms, and it left me in no doubt that Kay had chosen to pass her spirit into his body.

I loved this unusual story from Ben Miller about his cat, Cilla. It seems that not only can our pets come back to us in a new body, but they can also come back with a fixed agenda.

I've always been scared of cats – well, not just scared, terrified! People laughed at me when I was young and would cross the road to avoid one, and I didn't even like walking next to a fence in case a cat leapt up just as I was passing. The idea of suddenly being confronted eye to eye with my nemesis was really frightening. My girlfriend, Kate, who's always been into new-age stuff, said that maybe I used to be Egyptian in a past life and had been killed because I accidentally hurt a sacred cat. Maybe she's right. I'd never hurt a cat in this life, I just don't want to be near one, and especially I don't like the idea of looking one in the eye. They have that slit thing going on with their pupils, and I really don't like that.

No, I was a 'dog man' through and through. Dogs were cool; dogs didn't stare at me the way cats did. I had a Staffie called Ringo, and I really loved that dog. Ringo had a great sense of humour. He'd like to hide and then jump out on me, laughing all over his little fat face. He'd put things in my bed, like wet bones, or soggy toys, and laugh about that too, when I'd shriek and jump out of bed. We had a great time together for ten years and I always felt fine when I was out with him, because I'm ashamed to say I taught him to chase cats. That one word, *cats*, would have him whipping himself up into a frenzy, looking all around for the offending cat. He never caught one and of course I'd never have let him, but I felt safer knowing the neighbourhood cats would always keep their distance when I was with Ringo. So, of course, I was always with Ringo. That's why, when he died, I was so devastated. He'd been my buddy and my protector, so we'd been very close. Without him I felt naked and defenceless again, just like I used to when I was a kid.

From that day it was as if the local cats were getting their own back on me. Everywhere I went there they were, skulking under cars and hedges, peering out at me with their slitty eyes, especially at night when their eyes would glow. Kate got fed up with it and so she hatched a plan. She really did think she'd come up with the plan all by herself, but I know different.

One night she was waiting for me in the flat with a little cardboard box with air holes in it. I was thinking that if it was a puppy in there it had to be a really small puppy. I was horrified when I peeled the lid back and there was a *cat!* I recoiled and then peered fearfully over the lid. It wasn't so much a cat as a tiny, bedraggled kitten. It was wet and shivering, and I have to admit I felt sorry for it, but, 'Take it back! Right now!' I demanded.

Kate told me she couldn't. She said it had been thrown in the canal and she'd rescued it. I wasn't sure I believed her. It seemed far too convenient a sob story to me, but she wouldn't budge. She said she'd take it to the RSPCA in the morning, but it was late, they were closed, and it would die if I chucked it out that night. So I told her that, so long as I didn't have to touch it or go near it, I'd let her look after it just for the night. She got it out of the box and dried it, then she gave it a tin of tuna and settled it in a big fluffy towel on her lap.

In the end I went and sat next to her, because the cat had gone to sleep. All I could see was the top of its head where it poked out between the folds of the towel. Kate insisted on taking it into the bedroom with us, and in the morning when I woke up it was snuggled up against my neck. I nearly freaked out, but even my fear wouldn't allow me to hurt the little thing. Kate had vanished from the room, and so for the next half-hour I lay there, frozen, with the furry bundle up against my neck. It woke up and didn't move, but started to purr. I'd never felt a cat purr before, and it was kind of a nice feeling. To cut a long story short, you've guessed it, that kitten got into my heart and we kept it. But I wasn't cured. It was only that cat that I liked. When I was out I still avoided other cats like the plague.

A few weeks later, Priscilla, as Kate had called the little black kitten, was ready to venture into the outside world. Kate and I intended to go out into the garden with her and keep an eye on her the first few times, but there were no real fences and so we were worried that she might run off and get run over before she got streetwise. I had a brain-wave and suggested we put Ringo's collar and lead on her. It was one of those collars where the spike of the buckle just punches a hole in the strap, wherever it fitted, so it wasn't such a crazy idea. The crazy thing was that when I got it out of the cupboard, Cilla sat up immediately, looking right at the lead and waiting for me to put it on, just like Ringo used to do! Cats don't do that! Anyway, it seemed to be working, so out we went, and she walked as nice as pie on the lead as if she'd always done it. It got weirder. Over the next few days I decided to take her out for a walk on the lead around the streets, and when I did it was almost like old times with Ringo.

Of course, eventually it happened. Another cat appeared in the garden the other side of a low wall from me, and I froze. With that, Cilla leapt up on the wall, growling and spitting and all her coat standing on end. The other cat legged it, vanishing around the side of the house in a flash! It was really strange, and to this day Cilla still won't tolerate another cat near me, whether she's on the lead or not.

Then Kate and I started to realize that Cilla plays with Ringo's old squeaky toys and lies everywhere he used to lie. I have a feeling my old boy, with his great sense of humour, thought it would be hilarious to come back as one of my arch-enemies! He could also have done it as a test of my love for him. Would I still accept him in the body of a cat?

I've heard many stories of people having their phobia cured, or at least a solution found to living with it, by their remembering their own past lives, but this is the first time I ever heard of the same thing happening through a dog coming back, and as a cat at that! Certainly, though, dogs, cats and horses do have a sense of humour. My first pony, Baloo, was a great comedian. He'd wait until someone new came into the yard and then pull the most ridiculous faces at them. He'd curl up his lips and twist up his muzzle, turning his head almost upside down and showing his teeth. People would naturally laugh, and the more they laughed, the more extreme his faces would become. More than once I found a perfect stranger collapsing with helpless laughter in front of Baloo's stable door.

Chapter 5

Animal Messengers

*'Nothing is more noble,
and nothing more venerable,
than fidelity.'*

– CICERO

What would make a loved one send a message through, or appear as an animal? I think spirits in general have quite a tough time manifesting in any physical way on the earthly plane, so it may be that manifesting through an animal may be easier. In the case of Katie Willis's dad, I think he just liked the idea of making his family laugh.

My dad was always a great joker. He was always teasing us kids and playing jokes on us. Sometimes it was like he was the kid and we were the parent, but I would never have changed him. He was the best dad ever. But things changed and Dad changed when he was 48 years old.

Since he was a kid Dad had been obsessed with homing pigeons. He loved those birds so much. He had become an expert on breeding them and was very proud of each and every one.

He took us kids into the aviary every night and talked to us about them, showing each bird to us and telling us all about its history, how he'd bred it and what races it had won. He told us all the different colours and all the different strains and how he'd learned to breed the best. He hated to sell any, although sometimes the aviary got too full and he'd have to, but he always checked up on the birds' new home and was very fussy about where they went. The only days he wasn't there for us were the days his birds were racing. Once they'd been released from wherever, Dad would start scanning the skies with his binoculars, waiting for the first speck to appear. His greatest nightmare was sparrowhawks. Sometimes when his pigeons were out he'd be up at dawn, watching and praying that he wouldn't see the classic sneaky approach of a hawk coming after his birds.

I wished everyone had a dad like mine, but then, like I said, when Dad was 48, tragedy struck him. His pigeons developed salmonella. One of them must have picked it up during a trip out, because Dad's birds were kept as squeaky clean as we were. He was heartbroken and tried everything to stop it, but one by one his precious birds died. Dad blamed himself, but no one could have cared for them better than he did, and we kept telling him that. Finally, and she would have had to be the last, Dad was left nursing his favourite hen, Cleo. That wasn't her real, fancy name, but that was what Dad called her. When she died I thought Dad would never stop crying. I know there are people who'd say it was only a bird, but not to Dad it wasn't. He'd spent the best part of his life carefully selecting and breeding strains of birds to create the ultimate, and Cleo was 'it'. When she died I guess he thought his happiness had died too. She was a very beautiful specimen, even to me, being a quite rare mosaic colour. This colour is like it sounds, made up of many different colours mixed together, and the result is unique and very pretty.

Dad went downhill after that very quickly, and it seems that his kind and happy nature had another side to it, the reverse of the coin. Within six months he was diagnosed with lung cancer, and two months after that, we lost him. I think he got cancer out of grief, and he never really tried to fight it, as if he wanted to leave. We were all devastated, of course, but we felt we'd lost Dad the day Cleo died, and that maybe he was happier now. A few months passed and we'd fought our way out of severe grief into a place where we could start to remember Dad the way he'd been before he lost all his pigeons.

One day I was sitting in the garden. Dad had torn down the aviary, swearing he'd never want to use it again, and in a fit of trying to forget through hard work he'd built a summer house where it had stood. I was sitting in that summer house thinking of Dad and wondering, as we all do when we lose a loved one, where he was and whether he was OK. Just at that moment I heard the classic rustling sound of a pigeon's wings as it came in to roost. Then I could hear its soft cooing. It was a wild one of course, or so I thought. The bird fluttered to the ground and walked around to the front of the summer house. It was a mosaic! I stared and stared at it, too scared to move and frighten it away, because I swear it was Cleo. Her markings were unique, and this bird was definitely a well-bred racer. I knew enough to recognize that fact. But, if that was the case, it should have had a ring on its leg. All top-quality racing pigeons have an identifying ring on, giving a unique serial number for that pigeon. But this bird had no ring. I stared harder, and as if it knew what I was doing the bird opened its wings and walked round in a circle, letting me see all its body markings. I would bet £1,000 that bird was Cleo, Dad's Cleo, and yet she was dead.

I watched her for about five minutes, still sure that if I went to get Mum, she'd fly off. She kept winking at me. Pigeons do that a bit, but this wink was slow, as if it had meaning. Eventually I got up and very carefully leaned down to pick her up, but she wasn't having it and flew up onto the roof. I ran and got Mum, but of course when we came back out there was no sign of Cleo.

Whatever anyone ever says to me, and however silly it sounds, I believe this bird was sent by my dad. After all, pigeons were used in the war to ferry messages from resistance fighters in France back to England, so what better way for my dad to send us a message from the other side than by pigeon? It has a certain poetry to it, doesn't it?

A friend of mine recently lost his dear wife, and one of my best friends, to cancer. He was distraught and really wanted a sign from his wife that she still existed, somewhere. One day he was sitting on the bed she'd died in, gazing at the little hand-bell that was on the top of the covers. He'd given it to his wife in her last few days, when she was weak, so that she could ring it if she needed anything. He sat staring at the bell and willing his wife to please, please ring it, to prove to him that she was still around. Nothing happened for the longest time, and he was starting to despair.

His wife had absolutely adored their cat, and had a very close relationship with her. My friend heard the cat padding up the stairs at that point and really didn't want it to come into the room and disturb the moment. But the cat came in, paused for a second, then jumped onto the bed. Then she batted at the bell, just once, quite hard, enough to make it tinkle, and then she left the room and went back downstairs. It seems obvious and appropriate to me that, because she was not able to ring the bell herself, my friend asked her cat to do it for her.

Peter Ellis sent me another story about a pet who brought through a message. Oddly enough, this is another bird.

When I was a kid my nan and granddad had a grey parrot, which was of cause called Polly. Polly was an African grey and, as I know now, they are the best talkers. I was a little intimidated by Polly as a kid, because she had this (to me) huge scary beak and beady eyes. I was always sure she was going to bite me, but she never did. She was very good at impersonating, too, so I never knew if it was Granddad, Nan, my parents or Polly calling to me. Whenever someone like the milkman would knock at the door, Polly would shout, 'Who is it?' in Nan's voice. The person would naturally call back, 'It's the milkman!' Polly would repeat, 'Who is it?' and, if the caller was new, he would assume that some old deaf lady was calling out to him and keep answering louder and louder until someone put him out of his misery. It used to make me laugh, but I still looked at Polly with some mistrust.

Anyway, some years later we lost both Nan and Granddad within weeks of each other. They were in their 80s and, it seemed, didn't want to live without each other. It was very sad, and my dad was very sad, of course. The next thing I knew, Polly was installed in our house. Of course parrots live a very long time, and so we had to look after her. She was soon yelling out, 'Who is it?' to all our callers, and she'd keep visitors entertained for hours impersonating them. She'd start off by saying something in their voice, they'd laugh, she'd copy their laugh, and before you knew it everyone was crying with laughter. I realized Polly wasn't so bad after all.

One evening we were sitting in the living room. Polly's cage was covered with her night-time blanket. We had to do that or she'd spend all evening impersonating everyone on the TV! Mum and Dad were talking about Dad's parents, and how they were missed, when Polly suddenly started talking in Granddad's voice. We all looked at each other in amazement. First, she never talked with the blanket over her cage, and second, she had rarely spoken in Granddad's voice since he'd died. Then we were even more shocked, because Polly was saying stuff we'd never heard before. It went something like this.

'We're OK. We're happy. Look after Polly, and have a good life.'

Dad ran over and snatched the cover off the cage, startling poor Polly, who looked totally innocent. We'll never know for sure to this day if Granddad somehow used Polly to give us a message, but I think he did. She never spoke in his voice again.

They say that parrots are as intelligent as dogs and cats, so it's surprising we don't get more stories about them.

Perhaps that's because birds who have escaped life in a cage don't want to hang around! This story reminded me of another anecdote I was told recently by my friend, Rosemarie Davies. A friend of hers used to have a parrot which was allowed a lot freedom and was very attached to its owner, whom it used to call 'Mummy'. When this lady died it was in the times when coffins were left open in the parlour so that family members could pay their respects and say goodbye. The parrot was also allowed to be there to say goodbye, and when the coffin lid was shut, the bird said, 'Mummy gone to sleep.' How could this bird have understood and voiced the concept of someone 'going to sleep' or dying, unless it was sentient? Birds like parrots and budgies are said to be just mimics, unable to make rational statements formed by their own intelligence, like this one!

Christy Cooper sent me this story about her brother and a dog.

I live pretty much out in the 'boonies', and have to drive down a long, winding dirt road to get home. It's worth it, though, when you get there, because the place is so peaceful. Colorado is one of the most beautiful places in the world, if not *the* most beautiful, in my opinion. My brother Pete and I inherited the house and land from our parents, and we lived there (not always in perfect harmony, but always with love) for the next eight years after they died. Pete used to joke and say I'd never find a husband, and he'd never find a wife, stuck out in the backwoods, but I never cared; I loved the place and never wanted to leave it. We had just one neighbouring family and that was fine, too. Their daughter was Megan, my best friend, and we used to go to work in the city together every day.

Pete used to say I should get a dog. He started worrying about the times when I was alone at the house, sometimes all night if he was off partying. Much as I loved animals, however, I preferred to leave them wild, and besides it wasn't fair to a dog to leave it all day when we were both at work. Pete used to counter with the fact that he sometimes did night shifts and so the dog wouldn't always be left, but I managed to talk him out of it. Every time we went to a mall where there was a pet store, though, he'd 'Ooh' and 'Aah' over the pups in the window, trying to emotionally blackmail me into taking one home. I was getting used to the idea that one of these days he'd actually turn up with one and I'd have no choice in the matter.

I wish now I'd given in to him – well, in a way I do, because I lost my dear brother a year ago. He was killed in a freeway accident. I was in a state of shock for weeks, and because Pete's work hours had been so irregular, it was too easy to keep expecting him through the door. Eventually I adjusted, with Megan's help, and was able to go back to my job after a lot of sick leave.

One day, a few weeks later, Megan and I were driving back up the dirt track when we saw a dog standing at the side of the road. He looked like an English pointer, and we couldn't imagine what he was doing out there. Megan wanted to stop, but although the dog looked calm and kind enough, I'd once stopped to help another lost dog and it had attacked me, forcing me to jump back in my car and hightail it. Besides, I told Megan, it didn't look lost or upset. It was just standing there, gazing solemnly at us as we drove by.

I figured it was out with some walkers or something and was just waiting for them to catch up. But the next day it was still there, or there again, I'm not sure which, but still I wouldn't stop the car. I think I was being stubborn. I hadn't let Pete get me a dog, so I wasn't going to have this one. However, the third day was too much for me. I let Megan pull over and get out of the car. I was still too scared of being bitten. She walked cautiously over to the dog, cooing softly at him. He wagged his tail and then, to my surprise, he walked around her and stared at me, where I still sat in the car.

'He wants you to get out,' said Megan.

'No way,' I said, 'Don't be crazy.'

Megan reached out and took hold of the dog's collar. 'He's wearing a tag.'

Well, of course he was. You wouldn't get a pure-bred dog like that wandering around without a tag.

'Is there a number?' I asked, pulling out my cellphone.

There was no answer. 'Megan. Is there a number?' I repeated.

I looked at her, and she was looking back at me, a stunned look on her face, 'You have to see this.'

Sighing with frustration, I finally got out of the car and walked over. Megan was holding up the tag for me to see. The dog huffed amiably at me as I bent down to read the tag. There was no number, no address, just one single word, PETE.

I blinked. The dog was called Pete!

A tingling sensation travelled from my toes to my nose and I knew I had to take this dog home. I grasped his collar and led him over to the car. 'In,' I said. He jumped in, clambered into the back and sat on the seat, looking straight ahead through the windscreen, as if to say, 'Well, come on then. Let's go home.'

Thinking he was a valuable dog that someone would be missing, we called around, but no one ever claimed him. Pete lives with me to this day, and by now I don't know how I ever got by without him. I'm not saying Pete was my brother reincarnated, because obviously the dog must have been born before Pete died. I'm not saying anything. I'm just telling you what happened.

I have no doubt that this was more than coincidence. When you add together the fact that Pete tried to get Christy to buy a dog for so long, and that this dog was not claimed, and was carrying the name Pete, you have to conclude that Pete (the dog) was sent by Pete (the brother) to take care of his sister.

Butterflies are often thought to be messengers of the spirit world; this story from Graham Porter is one more example of their mystical power.

When my girlfriend Anna died, it was a terrible shock, despite the fact that she'd been terminally ill for months. I'd met her at a fairground and had been instantly captivated by her free spirit and her love for every living thing. It seemed so tragic that she should die so young. She was just 28. We'd had plans. We were going to get married, have a house with a picket fence, two dogs, a cat and four kids. It was hard for me to give up on that vision. But four years later I met Tracie, and my life started over again. Within two years, we'd bought our first home together and started planning for the future. There was just one problem. I'd never told Tracie about Anna. Somehow I thought she might be upset that I'd once loved someone else and been going to marry that person. I worried that Tracie might feel second best, although of course she wasn't.

In the end, however, my conscience wouldn't let me be, and I decided to tell her. So, one June day when we were sitting on the tiny front porch, the air very still, I knew this was the time. It was very quiet. There was no one about but us. As I'd feared, Tracie took it badly and started with all kinds of questions. Who did I love best? Did I still yearn for Anna? Who would I have chosen if she was still alive? I fumbled with answers, wanting to be honest and not wanting to say the wrong thing, which I inevitably did, and Tracie started crying. I felt helpless and she sagged against me, sobbing. She wasn't mad at me, and maybe it would have been better if she had been, she was just hurt and scared, as if I'd taken her security away.

Suddenly, down from the blue sky, a fluttering cloud started to descend. At first I didn't understand what it was, then I saw it was a crowd of bright blue butterflies. They came down to us and started to land on both me and Tracie. At first I was scared to move in case they flew off, but they showed no sign of it, just sitting there, their wings slowly opening and closing. Most of them were on Tracie, and I gently turned her head so she could see. She sat up, startled, and still they stayed on her. We were transfixed, and as we counted them we discovered there were 28 of them, the age Anna had been when she died.

I felt these butterflies were an omen, a signal that Tracie and I were perfect together and she shouldn't worry any more. I had loved Anna, but now I loved Tracie and that was that. They stayed with us for about ten minutes and then took off as one, spiralling up into the sky and finally vanishing. I had a thought – something I'd once read and pointed out to Anna when she was still alive. I got on the internet and then called Tracie indoors. On the screen was a photo of some bright blue butterflies – the same ones from the garden. And their name? ... Anna Blue.

These insects are fascinating because they metamorphose from sometimes garish and often vilified, caterpillars, into beautiful butterflies, and so are symbolic of the death of our corruptible body and the ongoing survival of the transformed, eternal soul.

I'm finding more and more stories about crows, which has been a bit of a surprise, really. Crows are not the most beautiful birds, and in some circles they're considered a pest. It just goes to show how little we really understand the animal spirit. This crow story comes from Somerset healer Ron Tropman.

A few years ago, international healer Bill Harrison and I were treating a man called Bob, who had a brain tumour. Bob would visit Bill on a Monday, then come and see me at home a couple of times a week to take advantage of my

Usui Reiki treatment. Bob and I became friends, and his wife would drop him off, then pop off to work, and Bob would sit and chat with me for a couple of hours.

Sadly, Bob's condition deteriorated after a time, and he ended up in hospital, where I went to visit him. During my talks with Bob, one of the things we discussed was our fears, and I told him about my fear of birds, especially large black ones.

A few days later I was woken up at 4 a.m. because there was a banging noise coming from the lounge. I got up and went to investigate. When I went into the room there was a huge black crow outside my patio window, attacking it with its beak and claws. I couldn't believe it. I tried to scare the bird away, but he kept coming back. Later that day I found out that Bob had passed away at the same time the crow had attacked my window.

The following morning I was woken again at 4 a.m. by the same thing. I decided to cover the window with a plastic sheet, just in case the crow could see his reflection and was attacking that. It didn't work, and the crow attacked the plastic sheet covering the window just as violently as he had the glass.

During the day the crow would sit on the telegraph pole outside the house and watch every move I made, and then attack the window early every morning. On the day of Bob's funeral the crow stopped and disappeared, but on the first anniversary of Bob's passing he started again. This time I walked outside and said, 'I know you're here, mate, now please sod off and stop attacking my window!' To this day the crow has never come back.

It's nice to know that the spirit world has a sense of humour! Obviously Bob found it very amusing to communicate with and yet tease his friend by returning in the form of the very bird that Ron feared most.

There was an amazing animal healer and communicator called Sue Smith, whom I was lucky enough to have had on my chat show many times. Her messages were of such importance to her that Sue would struggle to the studio even while in the throes of a bad lupus attack, and would have to partially cover her face, such was the state of her illness. Among many other things, Sue had a special connection to crows and their collective souls, and she could bring through amazing messages and information from the animal kingdom. She rescued all animals and never turned any away from her small sanctuary, but she specialized in rescuing and rehabilitating members of the crow family.

Sue died a few years ago and her loss has been keenly felt. When she was dying, Sue's bedroom would be visited by wild crows if the windows were left open. Sue was buried in her garden, her most sacred place, but before she died she wrote her own eulogy, which was read out at a friend's house in the presence of all her friends and colleagues. At the end of the eulogy Sue promised to stay in communication with them all from the other side. She told them they would know it was a genuine message from her because they would hear either owls calling in the daytime or crows calling in the dark. At the moment that these words were read out, a flock of thousands of crows flew low overhead, doing low-level flypasts just over the heads of the people gathered there. They say the sky was dark with them. There was not a soul present who remained untouched by the sight, or wasn't convinced that Sue had used her crow friends to send them the strongest message of all – *I am still here.*

When I got sent this other story about Sue and crows from Rosemarie Davies, I felt I had to include it here.

We chose Digby from an RSPCA overspill centre. He was the only one in a litter of tabby kittens with a white underside, and we thought that little bit of white would be a help on the road on dark nights. Poor Digby had a lot of trials to endure, and as my husband Gwynne and I are healers, we often seem to have desperate animals come into our lives. During his life Digby suffered from bone-thinning (to the extent that the vet said he'd never seen its like before), a broken pelvis and a nasal polyp caused by a seed going up his nose. All of these things Digby endured with immense courage and fortitude. Finally, though, despite all our care, there came a problem that even our little trooper with the heart of a lion wasn't able to overcome.

It seems that a lot of cats who have had a fractured pelvis at some time during their lives end up with a paralysed bowel, and so it was with Digby. We got him over the problem once, but eventually he ended up at the vet's, a drip attached to his poor little paw. I really didn't want to lose him. By then our dear friend Sue had died, and that day, when I went out of the back door, I was confronted by a large black crow standing on the step, regarding me solemnly, its head on one side. It wasn't at all afraid of me; it made eye contact with me and held it. I knew that Sue had sent the bird to warn me that Digby's time was up, and when the phone rang it was no surprise to find that the vet was calling to tell me that there was nothing more that could be done for Digby. Knowing that Sue had come to me through the crow, I was able to accept his passing better than I would have done otherwise.

We brought our brave boy home and buried him in his favourite spot in the garden. As we covered him over, four crows flew low over our heads, confirming to us that Sue had sent the one to our back door, and that she was ready to receive Digby into spirit with her.

It was a privilege to have shared the life of a beautiful, sentient being such as Digby. His grave has a stone circle around it with a picture of an angel inside, and there is a plaque that reads: 'Digby Davies. June 1999 – May 2008. BRAVE HEART' – for that is what he was.

It's fascinating how many times birds are used by spirits. I wonder if they're chosen because flight is so magical to us, and perhaps that makes us feel a little closer to God's own flying emissaries – angels.

Chapter 6

Telepathic Pets

Just after I left school I took a job in a boarding kennels for a while. Some of the dogs would bark and bark, and who could blame them, suddenly separated from their pack and thrust among a lot of strange dogs, unable to have any freedom? Of course they didn't know if their owners were ever coming back for them, but I started to notice quite soon that the day they were due to be collected they'd suddenly snap out of their depression and start bouncing around. The aggressive ones would turn pensive and a little abashed, as if they expected to be scolded by their owners for their misbehaviour, and the barkers would go quiet and sit, expectant, ears cocked. This wasn't just the odd dog, it was every dog.

I love this story sent to me by Lisa Avery.

Here is the story of the horse we called Freckles Kate. My husband and I went to look at Kate as a broodmare for our horse-breeding programme. We'd researched her pedigree and performance record, and knew she would be the best bred and nicest broodmare in our programme. We fell in love with her on the spot. She was a big bay mare with a big white star, gorgeous big brown eyes and strong bone and muscling. Kate came to live with us. She was 18 years old and had been without a foal for a year or so, and we thought it might take her a while to actually conceive, so we started breeding her in April. In May she showed as in season again, but when we took the stallion to her she wouldn't stand for him. An ultrasound confirmed our suspicion: she had taken on the first breeding. We followed up with many more ultrasound examinations to be sure that all was progressing normally, and our vet even did foetal sexing to see that it was a filly, although he had a little difficulty doing it. We were all so excited!

The next spring, in March, Kate gave birth to twin fillies who didn't survive the birth. It was heartbreaking for all of us. Having lost foals before, we knew that normally the best thing was to get right back to it, so we gave Kate some rest and then bred her again later that spring. She took, and all was well, until the autumn when she lost the foal. So the following year we bred her back. She was in great health and conceived easily, just as before. Into the autumn she was really looking pregnant and settled and we were so excited, but again, she lost the foal.

We called our dear friend, teacher, animal communicator and healer, Val Heart, to talk about Kate. I told her that

I felt very confused because by all appearances Kate was healthy and happy. So, we 'touched in' to talk to Kate together, and found her heart was still holding on to the twins that hadn't survived birthing. My heart went out to her. Whenever we lose a horse we lose a family member, and we all grieve. So Val and I talked about the situation and possible healing solutions, and together we came up with an idea.

The next day my husband and I took Kate to a special quiet grassy area with big pine trees, and we held a ceremony to help Kate's fillies pass on, and to help Kate let go. We gently explained to her that as she held those foals close she left no room for new life, and that it was OK for her to let go of the fillies, that we were there with her and that they were ready to go. Then we gently massaged her belly and made big sweeping motions (similar to birthing) from her belly to her flank, to her tail, and spoke about birthing the fillies and letting them go. I could even see them playing at her feet, before they loped into the heavens together. She could see them too, and then she looked at us, took a deep breath, and started to graze peacefully.

The amazing thing is how we could actually *see* the foals, and see them go, and see her belly physically/energetically change! She became lighter physically and mentally, and her heart was happier and full of love again.

The next spring Kate conceived easily, and gave birth to a beautiful filly for us. She is now bred back again and living happily in our pasture with her other broodmare friends. We are thankful to Val, and to Kate, and to all the angels who have helped us along the way.

That story really touched my heart. I could easily picture the poor mare and the sadness when she kept losing her babies. I could really see the scene when they were released. What a wonderful story!

When I got this following letter from Mimi Lawrence about her tortoise, I was amazed. It just goes to show that just because an animal isn't fluffy and cuddly, that doesn't mean they don't have some soul inside.

Of all the animals I've ever owned, I never expected that the closest link I'd have with one would be with a tortoise! I'd had dogs and cats and loved them dearly, of course, but I only had a surface connection. Now that I know what I know, maybe I'll be different with my next indoor pet. After we got Joey, the tortoise, I learned a whole new closeness with an animal. I'd talk to that little reptile as if he were a person, telling him all my troubles. His slow energy was somehow very calming.

It didn't take me long to realize that whenever I went to feed him, he'd be standing right there at the tray. It's not as if tortoises are renowned for their speed, either! I told my husband Jay, and of course he just laughed and said either Joey could hear me coming or that it was because I fed him at the same time every day. I knew he didn't hear me coming, because he would never have beaten me to the tray if he was at the other end of the garden and only set off then, and I didn't always do it at the same time either. Jay was wrong, and I set out to prove it with a series of experiments. Not only did Joey always get to the tray before me, whatever the time of day, but he didn't get there when Jay took him the food. So it seems that Joey's link was only with me, and I really felt that he was able to read my mind.

That certainly was an interesting one. Tortoises are very long-lived, of course, and I think this is why they're perhaps quite spiritually advanced. They must experience a lot in their lifetimes. The way Mimi describes Joey makes me picture him as a sort of wise little Buddha, with calm, gentle energy, never in any rush to get anywhere.

I was very pleased to get sent the following story from James Ford. When you read it you'll agree with me, I think – this is a very important case indeed.

My dog Moxy is a funny-looking little thing. She resembles a fox, but has patchy-coloured fur. She's a bit of a scruff, to be honest, but so cute. Whenever I was on my way home my from school, my mom would say Moxy would always know because she would jump up at the window and whine. I always thought that meant Moxy was telepathic, but someone told me she could probably just hear the sound of my bike as I turned the last few corners before I got there, which was a bit disappointing.

When I was 18 I left home and went away to university, leaving Moxy for the first time. I left Mom, too, and she claimed to be more upset than Moxy was. I missed them both but I was only about 50 miles from home, although it's true I rarely made it there, what with the high price of gas. So Mom worried a lot.

She said it was tough, because with me at university it was like I was nothing to do with her, and she never knew if I was looking after myself, or where I was, or if I were home safe or not.

At first Moxy missed me badly, Mom said, and would pace around at the time I used to get home, jumping up and down at the window and fretting for ages, and never really settling for the night. But then, after one afternoon when she'd sat very still for a long time, apparently deep in contemplation, Moxy's behaviour changed. She'd still, at some point every afternoon or evening, react as if I were coming home, but after the usual display she'd just get down from the window and go and lie down quietly, sighing in contentment and quite relaxed. At first Mom thought Moxy was just confused and hearing someone she thought was me coming down the road. Until, that is, we slowly put two and two together.

We started realizing that when I spoke to Mom on the phone and she asked me what I was up to, the times I'd said I was just home were the same times that Moxy displayed the new behaviour. We decided to run some experiments and, sure enough, when I started calling Mom to signal that I was home (just letting it ring a couple of times to save money), it would be about five minutes after Mom would notice Moxy getting wound up. After racing around for a bit, by the time I'd call she was always settled back down and calm.

We figured out that Moxy was happy so long as she knew I was home safe, even if it was in another home. Moxy was signalling to Mom that I was home safe and she could stop worrying. It proved so accurate that from then on Mom just had to watch Moxy to know that I was home safe ... but any ideas of staying out all night on the sly became a problem!

I was really excited by this story. I've heard of many cases of pets who seemed to know when their owners were coming home having been disproved or discredited by people saying that dogs have super-sensitive hearing and can hear and recognize their owner's car from miles away. In this case that wasn't what was happening at all.

Jodie Wallis, in her story, tells of another telepathic connection, but hers was with a cat. In her case, she might have sometimes wished Moyles wasn't quite so accurate.

I got my cat, Moyles, when he was just a kitten and I was five years old. He grew into a big cat, but he was soft as butter. Part Persian, ginger and white, and very fluffy, he was a striking figure. Poor old cat used to get dragged everywhere with me. I used to dress him up in my doll's clothes and wheel him round in a pram. Luckily he was a bit of a couch potato and so I don't think he minded that too much. But I guess he hated the way I scuppered his hunting instincts. He never had much luck tracking birds or mice as I was always hot on his tail. I used to take him to bed with me as well and cuddle him like a teddy. On reflection I did treat him a bit like a toy, which was a bit unfair of me.

However, now that I recently started dating, Moyles is getting his own back. He's decided to become my 'boyfriend monitor'. Mum says maybe he can read auras or something, or maybe he just knows what *she's* thinking. I think that's more likely, because any time I bring home a boy Mum isn't going to like the look of, maybe a Goth or someone well-studded, or even one who's just a bit old for me, Moyles just won't have it. He hides behind chairs, which isn't easy for a big ginger-and-white fluff-ball, and leaps out as they're walking by, snaring them around the leg, scaring the life out of them and quite often sinking in his teeth or claws. It's weird as he's usually such a gentle cat. Naturally I don't see the boys for dust after that, and Mum just has this smug smile on her face. Maybe one day I'll bring someone home and Moyles will curl up on his lap – maybe then I'll know who my husband is going to be, and so will Mum.

Now that I think about it, this kind of cat could be quite an advantage. Anyone who's had a string of disastrous relationships would find him very useful. Also, imagine in business if you could have your cat weed out the sheep from the goats, so to speak. It could save you a lot of money.

Jackie Knowles's dog's ability to connect with her in dreams literally saved him. This is the first story of its kind that I've ever read. It's quite a remarkable tale. We all know that dogs can dream, and are told that our dreams are just the sorting-through of the day's events, but I never heard of a dog that could interact with his owner's dream before!

I've never been in the slightest bit psychic and really I was a bit of a sceptic about the whole thing. I didn't even do horoscopes, so it never crossed my mind that a person and a dog might be able to communicate through thought alone – that all sounded a bit weird to me.

It all started one day in 2001 when I went to collect my new puppy. He was a beautiful Weimaraner, a lovely 'ghost grey' colour. I'd fallen in love with him at first sight. Pal, as I called him, was my very first dog, and I was so proud and determined to do everything right. I read reams of books and made sure he had the perfect food, the perfect training, the perfect toys and bed – perfect everything, really, and he was, totally, the perfect dog. I knew (from all the books) that Weimaraners could be difficult to train, so I was sure to sign up for the top classes, and we started to become a brilliant team. Never having had a dog before, I hadn't realized how wonderful they are as companions. As Pal grew and we bonded, I started taking him for longer and longer walks, so I got fitter, too. We trekked across Exmoor and then finally across Dartmoor, and that was where it all came unstuck. The moors are huge, largely wild open spaces and, especially on Dartmoor, the weather can close down really fast.

The only small issue me and Pal had was that he didn't always come to call, or not immediately. It was just exuberance, but I'd been warned that one day it would get him into trouble, and it did. We were out on Dartmoor and we'd been walking for hours, stopping for lunch in the lee of a tor. I was just starting to think about how great it would be to get back to the place I was staying and sit down to a hot dinner. I'm sure Pal was dreaming of a warm bed by the fire, too. It was a nice day, really, cold but crisp, and of course we were very warm from all the exercise. We were probably only two miles from safety and warmth when it suddenly started to snow. At first it was pretty, but then it got really heavy and the wind blew up. Before I knew it I couldn't see the trail any more, and I was only safe because of my trusty compass, but Pal didn't know that. He started chasing the snow and got further and further away from me. His gorgeous colour didn't help as he blended in so well. I was trying to get him to stay close and then the worst thing happened. A rabbit – which had obviously been trying to pluck up the courage to make a break for home – shot out of cover right under Pal's nose. He chased after it, despite my screams to come back, and the two of them vanished into the whiteout. You can imagine the rest. I yelled and called myself hoarse, Pal never came back, the snow got worse, the cold started to bite, and I had no choice but to try and get back to the pub without my Pal.

I made it back but I was desolate. I wanted Search and Rescue to go look for my dog, but it was hopeless in the dark and, as they said, he could be miles away by then. After a sleepless night the day broke clear and the snow had stopped. I tried to find my way back to the spot where

I'd lost track of Pal, but the snow had obliterated all the tracks. I stayed at the pub for two weeks in all, and every day I looked for Pal, but I never found a trace.

I cursed a friend who'd advised me not to get him micro-chipped, as she said some dogs were made ill by it. Everyone said I should give him up, and that there was no way he'd ever find his way home from there. I went home, reluctantly, but Pal was never out of my thoughts for long. The worst thing was not knowing what had happened to him, and also blaming myself. If only I'd been a better trainer. If only we hadn't gone there that day. If only I'd had him microchipped, although that would only be any good if he turned up at a vet's and they checked for one. I'd been a bit of a loner before I got my dog, and now I was alone again. I got really depressed. Every evening when I came home from work I expected Pal to be sitting on the doorstep, but he never was.

Then, just when I'd given up hope, I had a dream. I dreamed of Pal. He was in a big cosy kitchen with a range. He was sitting up, not looking very relaxed, and whining. A woman appeared, and then, as Pal got up to greet her, I could see he had a heavily bandaged, maybe plastered, leg. I was so shocked I woke up. Could it possibly, possibly be that Pal had actually come to me in a dream? I didn't understand it, but I wanted to believe it more than I'd ever wanted to believe anything in my life. I decided to try the vet's in the vicinity again. There were so many, because I had no idea how far Pal had roamed. I'd called all of the ones around where we'd been with no result, but then I decided to try something new. I sat down very quietly and cleared my mind. It wasn't easy, but then into my head popped a sign. It said, 'Tor Cottage'.

I was onto something, I just knew it!

Have you any idea how many Tor Cottages there are in Devon? A lot! It took me several weeks of trying, phoning every post office in every village, but eventually I found him. A wonderful woman called Jean Nightingale had found my poor Pal the day after I'd lost him. He'd fallen off a rock in the snow and broken his leg.

I thank God every day that she found him, or he would have died for sure. Jean was happy to have the vet bills paid, and she was even happy to hand him back, because she said he had never been happy with her. I'll never know for sure what happened between me and Pal, but I know he looks at me kind of funny sometimes, and all but winks.

That amazing story of a pet finding a way to be reunited with his owner reminded me of what happened with our lovely cat, Felix. He was a wonderful, black, fluffy cat with the most vivid, big green eyes. He had a way of making his meow sound like 'Hello.' We had him for several years and then we moved house to a place out in the countryside. We had of course been warned that we mustn't let the cat out for several days, or we'd risk losing him for good. We had him shut in a basket for the actual move, but eventually of course we had to let him into the house.

Our son Phillip was only about seven years old at the time, and although we gave him strict instructions not to let Felix out, of course at his age he was so interested in running around in the new open spaces that he forgot. He opened the door without checking for the cat, after we'd only been there about five minutes, and whoosh, off went Felix, tail up, running for his life. He ran straight down the garden in the direction of the nearest road and vanished from sight. Phillip was crestfallen so we made light of it, but Tony and I thought that was the last we'd seen of our cat.

Between the new house and the old house were about five miles of open fields, but there would also be several main roads to cross on the way. We decided that we'd give him a couple of hours and then drive back down there and see if there was any sign. I had a quiet few moments to pass in our new paddock, and I sat and thought about Felix. He'd been gone about an hour by then and I was tempted to go out in the car and look for him. Then I had a vivid mental picture of Felix trotting along a field edge, but ahead of him was the first of the main roads. I decided to try and capitalize on the connection, if that's what it was, so I started sending thoughts to Felix. I sent images of us, of a nice warm fireside and his food bowl. In my mind's eye the vision changed and Felix stopped trotting and stood still.

I then tried to show him all the mice and voles he'd be able to chase if he came back to our new place in the country, as opposed to his life in our previous, now barren town garden. I tried to communicate all the great adventures he could have in his new space, and in my vision Felix turned around and started back the way he'd come. I was overjoyed as I really felt this was all real, and so I went back indoors and waited.

An hour later Felix came trotting back along the same path he'd bolted down two hours previously, and he never roamed again.

Rachael Doonar sent me this lovely little account from Australia. It's just a sign of an everyday connection between a dog and her owner. A sweet little tale.

I was sitting with my little mini-foxy [fox terrier] Peanut, and was thinking about how guilty I was feeling about not walking her very much. I then thought to myself while looking at her, *What is it you would like to do today, Peanut?* I instantly saw a tennis ball flying through the air in my mind's eye, and Peanut was wagging her tail and looking at me. I had to laugh out loud, as I knew how much she liked to retrieve the ball. I felt she'd communicated with me that she wanted to play fetch.

When we're in a state of grief, our pets can bring great comfort just by being there. In Wendy Storer's case, her mum and dad's dog was able to do far more than that.

When my mum died, because none of my family was at all religious or church-going, we arranged her funeral ourselves. My biggest contribution was to write her eulogy. I wasn't with her when she died and it was my way of saying everything to her that I needed and wanted to say. I shut myself off from the rest of the family to write it, but Paddy (Mum and Dad's much-loved Labrador) came into the room with me. I sat down and wrote for about two or three hours, pouring my heart onto paper. Of course I cried and cried while writing, and felt much better for it. It never struck me as strange that, while I was writing, Paddy stayed at my feet, also crying. He never usually whined or whimpered, but on this day he did just that. I honestly believe he had somehow connected with my emotions. Whether he was crying because I was, because of his own loss or because he understood that it was about Mum it's impossible to know, but there is no doubt that this was heartfelt and I have no doubt that Paddy was aware of the emotional pain in that room.

Soon after that I was walking Paddy with my two youngest children, then aged two and three. They'd grown up with Paddy and were not at all frightened of dogs, but on this particular day a large, quite aggressive-looking dog came running over to us. I could feel the children's fear immediately, but before I could react Paddy placed himself between the dog and my children and stood his ground, growling until the other dog went away. There is no doubt in my mind that Paddy was protecting my babies and me from danger. I remember feeling very proud of him and utterly grateful, because I was strung out and emotionally weak and he did all the thinking and reacting for me.

A few months later my dad went to the Philippines for several weeks to see an old friend. He left Paddy with me, and Paddy was just his normal, playful, happy self and showed no signs of missing my dad or being homesick. The day my dad was due to fly home, however, Paddy changed. He sat by the door and started to whine, like he was expecting someone to appear. When we worked it out, it appeared that this change in Paddy's behaviour coincided almost exactly with the moment Dad was getting on the plane in Manila. Somehow, Paddy knew that his best friend was coming back to him.

They say that energy travels, and that when we're in a state of grief our energy is low and weak. Animals are able to sense the energy of our emotions, easily as well as the top psychics do. Even if we're able to hide our emotions from our nearest and dearest human companions, animals are a different story. For instance, Paddy knew that Wendy would normally have instantly put herself between her children and the scary dog, but he also knew that on that day her energy was at low ebb and she needed his help.

Her second story below is quite different and shows a dog using his reasoning skills.

My dog nowadays is Bodger, a Labradoodle. The journey from my house to the park where we normally walk goes past an old stone wall. Bodger likes to walk between me and the wall, sniffing the wall all the way. The only exception to this is one stretch of the wall where it bows outwards. When we reach this stretch, Bodger always moves from my right side to my left and walks as near to the road as he possibly can (despite being normally quite spooked by loud traffic). As soon as the bowed stretch has come to an end, Bodger returns to my right side and walks happily along sniffing the wall. He repeats this ritual on the way home, in reverse. He obviously dislikes this stretch of wall for some reason and is quite obsessive about not walking next to it. I wonder if he senses a danger because it is a load-bearing wall with quite a lot of weight behind it.

These stories from Wendy show dogs who are so in tune with their owner that they appear either to be able to read their minds or are so self-aware that they recognize the danger to themselves from an overhanging brick wall. Either way, these are not the actions of insensate animals.

In the first instance Paddy is either grieving, which scientists might say a dog is not capable of doing, or he sympathized and empathized with Wendy's grief. In the second incident Paddy read and recognized weak energy in his usually strong leader and took over when danger threatened. In the third incident he seemed to be able to telepathically connect with his owner, although he was still thousands of miles away.

In the incident with Bodger and the wall, Bodger shows reasoning skills that should be beyond a dog – *That wall is leaning, and may collapse, so I shouldn't walk near it.* Here's another wonderful story from Alice Jean, my remarkable Texan friend who keeps Nubian goats.

I don't understand how a person can say, 'I'm not a cat person' or 'I'm not a dog person.' It makes no sense to me. You either love animals or you don't! Now, after saying that, I have to admit that many times I've said, 'I'm not a bird person.' Usually this will be when a friend is trying to talk me into having a caged bird in the house. In a cage! No. But with any kind of feathered thing, I don't want to touch them! They are perfectly beautiful outside flying around. Interesting things have taken place around me concerning birds. A humming bird, bigger than any I've ever seen, stopped two feet from my face and just looked at me for the longest time. I seemed to get a message about spiritual warriors. I have no idea if it was the bird, or an angel, or God giving me advice, or just my imagination. Humming birds are quite beautiful seen up close.

Now, buzzards! Who could say a buzzard is beautiful? I'm beginning to see their beauty, though, after some rather close encounters. A couple of years ago, as my dairy goats went out to pasture I settled into a lawn chair with my coffee and a book. It was a beautiful day. All at once I was startled as a buzzard zoomed over my head at low altitude. Then, from behind me, it rose up in the sky and out to the pasture, circling the goats and then came flying back overhead. *What is wrong with this bird*? I thought. Every time it came back my way, it was lower. Finally I put the book down and stood up to watch and make sure it wasn't threatening the goats at all. They didn't seem to even notice. Then I heard, in my head, *Check on Isabel*. As I got closer I realized that my goat Isabel was having her kids! In the pasture! That's what we have kidding pens for. *How did she fool me?* I grabbed some kitchen roll and trotted out there. Well, once the birthing has started it takes a while, so I stayed with her until all four kids were born. Of course I ended up carrying the kids back to the barn, in my big shirt, two at a time, and into the pen, with Isabel in tow. Silly, maybe, but I gave a wave to the buzzard when we got back and it flew off. That wasn't the end of it. The following year, last year, I let the goats out to the front pasture. Another beautiful day, so a book and mug of coffee and the lawn chair. Now I do have due dates, since my goats are registered Nubians. We always know what buck we bred each doe to, and a due date can mean five days earlier or five days later than the date itself. On this day I had kept one goat, Noreen, back from going out with the others because it was her due date, and she looked ready. The kidding pen has an outside yard so she could walk around and eat hay and not feel so confined. I settled my chair close by, expecting to have new kids any time. All at once a buzzard flew into the yard and settled on a branch not 20 feet from me. 'Now what do you want?' I said out loud. I didn't think I wanted the ugly thing so close to my Noreen. Guess what I heard? In my head, I heard, *Better check on Isabel.*

What? I had to walk around the side of the barn to get a view of the goat herd and, sure enough, Isabel was kidding! Again she'd fooled me! So off I go with the kitchen roll and the same routine of carrying back four kids! That Isabel had triplets once in her life and every other time it's been quads. I'm letting her rest now and be the granny of the barn. She deserves it. Now, the interesting part is this: I was telling my husband and oldest son my buzzard stories – I don't go telling these stories in public. Hubby and son began reminding me of something that happened many years ago, when we lived in a different house about a mile and a half from here. I had come home after dark with my four sons. Hubby was out of town. When I pulled the car in the driveway we could see something in the back of the garage on the workbench. A very big bird! I thought, *Let's get in the house and I'll see about it.* I didn't want my children to get hurt if this very big bird felt trapped. We noticed that it didn't move from where it was, and seemed to have a hurt wing that kind of drooped. I brought out a bowl of dog food (what do you feed a buzzard?) and a pot of water. In the morning both bowl and pot were empty, so I refilled them. This went on for several days until one day he/she was gone. My son is convinced that it must be the same family of buzzards that has set up home in the abandoned old house across the yard from our house, on our property. He's seen, in the attic of the old house, that they've made nests and are raising their young there. I see them standing on the edge of the opening to the attic sometimes, and the funny thing is that if I give a little wave, they nod their heads. How great is that? I wonder sometimes if there are, in the collective unconsciousness of buzzards, some memories of a kindness and dog food and water. *Or could these all be the same buzzard in new bodies?*

I was talking on the phone today to my friend, The Barefoot Doctor, and he told me this great story, which I immediately knew I had to include in this section.

Walter was a dog with the most incredible charisma and air of intelligence. One look into those eyes was enough to make you understand that animals have souls that are in many ways more evolved spiritually than ours. He was a gorgeous champagne-coloured dog that was half wolf, half husky, and when he appeared on my TV show he was billed as 'Walter, The Almost-Human, Taoist Dog'. Despite his obvious great physical power, Walter was very gentle and cuddly, always keeping his great strength in check unless he needed it to defend himself.

Walter meted out doggie wisdom to my viewers, and he was a very important part of my life. He never wore a lead and there was never any need. He patrolled his 'patch' in West Hampton with all the aplomb and assurance of a king.

The only time he got 'lost' was when I was in Spain. I can only imagine that Walter, back in England, was annoyed at my absence and thought he'd teach me a lesson by going walkabout. My poor PA, who was in charge of him at the time, was mortified at having to tell me she'd lost my dog, but after he'd been missing for 24 hours she rang me from the police station five miles from where we live, where she'd gone to report Walter missing. I was a complete mess, but decided to try and connect with him and see if I could find out where he was. I went into a meditative state and summoned an image of my dog, asking him, 'Where are you? Come on, show yourself and let us know where you are.' The image of his face in my mind smiled, as only a dog can smile. The phone rang ten minutes later. It was my PA. She could hardly speak because she was so dumbfounded. She told me that there she'd been, sitting in the police station, and Walter had just casually strolled in! He was filthy, with dirt and chewing gum and other unidentifiable gunge stuck in his coat, as if he'd been living rough, but apart from needing a bath, he was fine.

You have to ask yourself: How did he find her? How did he come to walk into that police station at that time? The only answer I can come up with is that he 'saw' the place by reading my mind, and decided the time had come to turn himself in.

Chapter 7

Clairvoyant Pets

'Ask the beasts and they will teach you the beauty of this earth.'
– St Francis of Assisi

One of our dogs used to see spirits, or that was what we assumed. She'd sit and stare at things we couldn't see, her eyes following whatever it was around the room. She never seemed spooked by whatever it was, and I never saw anything in that particular house, but Tony did smell pipe smoke sometimes, although no one in the house (living, that is) smoked anything at all.

Janice Seymour sent me this story of her dog and cat. I thought it was a great confirmation that not only can cats be connected to spirit, and not only can dogs be connected to spirit, but they can be connected to each other on a soul level too.

My dog Regis and my cat Portia were inseparable. We got them both together as tiny bundles of fluff, and they went everywhere together, slept together, investigated things together. Quite often it was hard to tell which one was the dog and which the cat. Regis played like a cat, and Portia sniffed around like a dog. So it wasn't all that strange, I guess, that they also started seeing spirits together.

It started one evening in 2004. We'd just moved into an old house with a bit of history, and as me and Jake, my husband, were both interested in ghosts and stuff, we were kind of hoping the old place might have a ghost or two. Regis and Portia weren't so keen! It was a really hot evening and we had no air conditioning, so we had all the doors and windows open. We were still hot, though. It was breathless, no wind at all, and the air hung heavy around us.

Suddenly I felt a shiver as a draught of cold, almost icy air swept around my ankles. It was really odd as none of the curtains was moving at all. At the very same second Regis, who'd been fast asleep on the rug, and Portia, who'd been right next to him, both jumped up in the air and spun round to face the stairs. Jake and I looked, too, naturally, but nothing was there. Regis growled and Portia hissed, both of them with their hackles up. This kind of thing happened many times, until eventually the animals started to almost ignore whatever it was. They resorted to just staring and following it with their eyes, but Jake and I never saw anything.

Years later Regis got a bit rickety, and didn't move so well. He'd still romp with Portia and the two of them would cuddle up together in the evening, but he was getting old. At 15 he was a good age for a dog, but of course Portia was still quite sprightly, cats generally living longer than dogs. She was very sweet with him, waiting if he got left behind and, when he didn't see too well, guiding him around. She didn't even moan when he ate her food by mistake.

Jake and I discussed what on earth we'd do if Regis died. How would Portia cope? Finally the day came, and Regis died in his sleep. We left him where he lay so that Portia might understand he'd gone, rather than snatching him away from her. She was completely disinterested in his body, which surprised me. I thought she might push him with her paw or something, to try and make him get up. But no, instead she went off into the garden, as if for all the world Regis was with her.

But by night she wasn't so happy. We'd had to take Regis's body away and she didn't seem to know how or where to go to sleep. Jake and I did our best and tried to comfort her, but she didn't want to know. Finally, at about 9 p.m., she suddenly jumped up and started meowing, looking towards the stairs, and we were put in mind of that first time they saw our 'ghost'.

Her meows got more and more excited and she went bounding up the stairs, as if she were chasing something.

Jake and I got up and followed her, but she was too quick for us and all we saw was the flash of her tail as she rounded the top of the stairs. By the time we got up there she'd vanished into the bedroom. We went in. We were staggered and pretty upset to see Portia lying stiff on the bed. She must have died in a second as we were still coming upstairs. Then we realized what had happened! Regis had come back for her!

How beautiful that this dog came back to collect his cat pal. These animals teach us humans a valuable lesson in getting along with others who are a bit 'different'. On a soul level there is no difference between us, and the world would be a better place if people were more like Regis and Portia.

Jessie Cambridge sent me another story of a spirit-seeing dog. She had an unusual and interesting way of verifying what he was looking at.

I got my dog, Barney, as a pup. He was a cross between a springer spaniel and a Labrador, black with piercing brown eyes. His eyes are amazing, golden brown with flashes of amber in them, and everyone remarks how they shine against his jet-black coat. He's always been very 'knowing', either taking a liking or a dislike to people from the word go. I often wondered if he could see their auras, and in the end I think I wasn't far off track. As a family we got very used to seeing him watching an invisible 'something' as it moved around the room. He'd wag his tail at it and usually the 'something' would end up leaving through the ceiling while Barney stared up at it, transfixed. Then after a few seconds he'd just turn and walk away, game over.

Sometimes Barney would actually get up on his hind legs and 'play snap' at midair as if he was trying to grab something. One or the other member of the family would comment, 'Hello, Barney's ghost-busting again.' In fact he started to develop the nickname, 'Ghost-busting Barney'. Or we'd all say at once, 'Who you gonna call? Our Barney!'

One day I read an article about orbs captured in photographs. It said that if there were spirits about, even if you couldn't see them, a digital camera would capture them as orbs. So I got a camera and prepared to capture some spooks. I didn't really think it would work, and sure enough for the next few weeks Barney didn't do any ghost-busting, or if he did I wasn't quick enough with the camera. But then, because I was observing him closely, I was able to spot the signs of an imminent ghost-hunt. Barney would stand there wagging his tail for no reason, as if he could sense something coming.

So, more prepared, I was able to get snapping. Much to my amazement, and that of the family, I started getting orbs in the photos right away. Sometimes he'd be surrounded by them.

Of course it's possible that as an animal sheds dander all the time, these orbs were actually scraps of Barney's hair and dust, especially if he was dancing around when the picture was taken, but given that his behaviour was so extraordinary, I'm inclined to believe they were real.

This next story made the hair on the back of my neck stand up, as it's one of the spookiest I've been sent. Sue McNeill has never forgotten this incident.

I was one of the lucky ones – I had a pony of my own from a young age. I was a huge fan of books like *Black Beauty*, and so I called my little dapple-grey mare Merrylegs, or Merry for short. She lived up to her name, and we spent many happy hours, just the two of us, roaming the lanes, fields and bridleways of Hampshire. I always felt safe with Merry, and after some trepidation my mum was relaxed about me disappearing with her for hours, too. She might not have been quite so keen if she'd known some of the adventures we had! Like one time I came across an old man in the woods who tried to persuade me to get off my pony and go with him. Merry seemed to immediately sense the danger, and although I would never have done what he said anyway, she left me no choice, rushing me away at a canter in the opposite direction, as if she'd seen a rattlesnake! Another time I tried to make her cross a ford, and although she usually went through water quite happily, she refused point-blank this time. Then, while I was still trying to persuade her, a car came through and got stuck, because the water was much higher and running much faster in the middle than I'd realized.

The day that really scared me, though, was one I *did* tell Mum about, because I needed her reassurance. We'd had a nice ride and I decided that we'd take a shortcut through Berry's Wood because the day was hot and the shortcut would take half an hour off the journey. It all started out all right as we set off across a meadow. The entrance into the woods lay diagonally across the grass, and was swathed in deep shadows cast by the big, low-hanging oak trees that marked the boundary between woods and open field. As we were about halfway across the field, Merry suddenly stopped dead. She refused to move at all and tried to turn round. My pony wasn't normally spooky, so I should have listened to her, but I was only 12 years old, so I suppose I can be excused.

I kept turning her in circles, forcing her ever closer to the edge of the woods, but by the time we were about 50 yards away, Merry started shaking. She was staring at the trees and quivering with fear. That did make me think, because she'd never done that before, so I let her stand still. After a few seconds I saw it. A smoky shadow detached itself from the genuine tree shadows, and started swirling across the field towards me and my stricken pony. We were both frozen with fear. The shadow was as black as night and it writhed and twisted its way across the grass. As it got closer the air around us began to grow cold, and the bright sun shining overhead only made the chill feel deeper as the shadow came closer. The darkness inched nearer until it was only a few feet from Merry's front hooves. I could see the sharp line it cut across the bright green grass, and beyond was stark, Stygian darkness that the sun couldn't penetrate.

I dread to think what might have happened if Merry hadn't shown more courage than me, whirling around quickly – though carefully enough that I didn't get tipped off – and setting off across the field at a gallop. I never looked back.

What on earth was this threatening black shape? There's something referred to as 'shadow people', but they're usually people-shaped and seem pretty harmless; this entity seems to have been very menacing and dangerous. Whatever it was, I'm glad Sue had Merry to take care of her.

The medical profession are now training pets, especially dogs, to seek out illnesses in people. There are dogs trained specifically to indicate the presence of cancer and diabetes in particular. There are also dogs and cats that have been known to tell their owners with diabetes that their blood sugar is out of balance, or their owners with epilepsy that a seizure is imminent. Just how they know this is a mystery. This next story of Alice's is a case in point.

About 15 years ago we were gathering our six cats in carriers to take them to the vet's office for spaying and neutering. One of the males was an outdoor guy, and when my hubby went to find him he actually came back to the house with a beautiful calico female, asking me where she came from. Neither of us had ever seen her before. She was just as calm as can be as he held her. We put her in a carrier just to hold on to her while I phoned the neighbour. It turned out she was a stray who'd shown up at their place about a month before, and they didn't want her. 'Not cat-people,' they said. That was fine with us. We took her to the vet's with the intention of keeping her.

When we brought the cats home from their ordeal, I suggested we leave the new one in the carrier in the kitchen until she got her bearings. We named her Rosa, but since then we mostly call her Pootie or Rosa MaCalico. I stayed around the kitchen that night and noticed that she just didn't seem bothered about being locked up at all. Even stranger, the other cats weren't curious about her. When I opened the door to her carrier, Rosa stepped out and stretched, and then wandered into the utility room to use the litter box. She came back and went to the food and water, and onto the couch for a nap! Talk about making yourself at home! I felt like I knew her, and she was always looking at me. She's the only cat that I've ever encouraged to sit on the kitchen cabinet. If I was fixing the coffee pot, she'd watch intently, as if she were learning a new skill. She'd lean forward to smell the coffee when I took the lid off the can, then up straight again and watch the rest of the procedure. I'd put a stop to allowing kitties in the bedroom after we got our new comforter. They were all young and picked at it until I thought we'd have feathers coming out. But, for some reason, we allowed Rosa in there. I loved being with her. Now I have to fast-forward to two years ago. I always sleep on my side, and Rosa would always climb on my hip, lightly 'knead', and rest there awhile before settling on the bed against me to wash herself and curl up to sleep. It was almost like she was putting me to sleep first. She's real motherly towards the other cats too. Two years ago this summer, though, Rosa started a rather bizarre behaviour. She'd get up on my hip as usual, but instead of lightly kneading right there, she'd reach down towards the bottom of my belly, closest to the bed. Balancing on my hip, she'd reach right down and actually pick at me through the covers. It didn't hurt so I'd let her carry on. Anyone who lives with and loves cats knows that if you stop them before they're finished with whatever's on their mind, they'll just keep going back to it until they *are* finished. Anyway, she kept on doing this every night.

I wasn't feeling real well that summer, and even made a doctor's appointment. I found out that I had a tumour the size of a tennis ball on my left ovary. Right there on the left side that used to be closest to the mattress, and right where Rosa had been picking at me. It wasn't until way after my surgery that I realized that Rosa's bizarre behaviour had stopped. It made me wonder. I do think that she was trying to help me and knew about that tumour. God, I wish they could talk – or even better, that I could listen and understand them more.

Rosa 'Pootie' MaCalico is still my 'baby'. Or is she my mother, come back to me? Most probably, in her next life, *she'll* be making the coffee.

Steve Rose sent me this charming tale about his cat.

My twin brother and I are mediums, clairvoyant healers. My brother started to give readings before I did. One day he gave me a reading for our twenty-second birthday. We sat in a bedroom with a candle between us and Chris used some tarot cards. We had one of Mum's cats in the room, who was sitting quite happily under the table.

Chris was doing very well when we noticed the cat had seen something in the room. It chased around and around like there was an invisible mouse or something. The cat was literally going up the walls and over the bed and around and around in circles. This went on for a good couple of minutes until finally the cat became frightened of whatever it was and buried his head in my lap, so hard I thought it would hurt his face. He was shaking and just wanted to cover his head. I comforted him, which helped, but he stayed in that position for the rest of the reading. My trousers were covered in a mixture of cat saliva and hair. It was funny until he became frightened and then we asked whatever it was to leave. He eventually calmed down and acted all cool and cat-like, as though nothing had happened.

I remember reading that a cat's brain is made up of primarily optic nerve. I think that on that day this nerve was working a bit *too* well for Mum's cat.

They say that dogs and cats only see the grey spectrum, so I wonder what ghosts might look like to them. It's not really surprising that animals see spirits, because their senses in general are much more attuned than ours. That's why they can sense things we can't, like bad weather coming. During the terrible tsunami that killed 150,000 people a few years ago, the only animals, wild or domestic, that were killed were those who were confined in some way.

My dog Sally had an amazing talent that made it seem as if she were using ESP. She could find balls. At first that might seem like the natural result of an amazing sense of smell, but the balls belonged not to me, but to children – any children – playing outside. Opposite our house there was a field smothered in bramble bushes and thick undergrowth. The neighbourhood kids were always playing outside, in those days of little traffic and no computers. Of course, every day a ball of some sort would end up being thrown, kicked or batted into the field, where it would prove impossible to find. Sally was so good at finding them that the kids would come and knock on the door asking, 'Can Sally come out?' I'd take her out and it wouldn't matter which area of the field it had gone in, or who had owned and touched the ball. I would just stand at the roadside and tell her, 'Find it!' Sally would rush off into the field with no directions from anyone and within minutes, sometimes seconds, she would emerge triumphant with the ball. She was a real hero to the kids.

Chapter 8

Wild Animals

'There are no wild animals until man makes them so.'
– MARK TWAIN

We don't often hear of the ghosts of wild animals, which might make you think that wild animals don't have a soul, but it's just that we're not often there to see them. There may be herds of ghost zebra roaming the plains of Africa, and hordes of spirit monkeys scaling the trees of the rainforests – who'd see them? And if anyone did see them, under that hot sun, they might be thought to be a mirage, or be put down as misty illusions among the steamy jungle trees. But I have managed to track down a few sightings, which are intriguing to say the least.

I couldn't resist this one. A ghost zebra? In Arizona? When it was sent to me, by Christen Martin, my first thought was that it sounded a bit ridiculous, but then I gave it some thought and decided to include it for reasons I'll expand on after the story.

Pets Have Souls Too

We'd had a great holiday in Arizona, visiting the mystical town of Sedona and gazing awestruck at the majesty of the Grand Canyon. We'd never realized that Arizona was so amazing, so full of wonders to behold such as the mountain-top town of Jerome, perched up high on the Mingus Mountain, or the myriad colours of the Painted Desert. But it seemed that the town of Phoenix also had something unusual to show us. Our motel was about a mile from the zoo, but it was far too hot during the day to visit it. Phoenix is a huge city, and while out in the desert – especially up mountains and in Sedona – it had been dry and hot, it had also been fresh, whereas in the concrete jungle of the city the heat bounced off the pavements and threatened to blister you just by looking at the heat haze. We had a lot of trouble finding our way around the city too, it was just too big. We spent ages driving around on what to us was the wrong side of the road, looking for a shopping mall. I'm sure there are many of them in a city that big, but we couldn't find one!

So we found ourselves quite late in the evening, driving past the zoo on our way back to the motel, just being happy we'd found our way back. As we passed the approach road, I saw something. It was quite a large animal, like a pony, and I just got a glimpse of its back end as it went charging round the bend, up towards the zoo. I have horses at home and the first thing that sprang to my mind was that someone's pony had escaped and was running wild on the road. I'd had a pony killed on the road too, so no way could I just ignore this one. Of course, as well as traffic there were other hazards for the pony, such as heat, scorpions and horse-thieves. So, although I had no idea what I was going to do with the pony once I caught it, I felt I had to try.

So this was how we came to find ourselves approaching Phoenix Zoo after it was shut, at about 10.30 p.m. one hot Arizona night. As we rounded the bend I could see the animal, and that was when I realized there were two of them! That wasn't the weirdest part, either. They were wearing pyjamas! Well no, obviously, actually they were two zebras. So now we had a different problem to contend with: two escaped zebras. Ideas whirled through my mind. We should back off and find a phone, call the zoo or the police or someone and let them deal with it.

Then we realized the two of them were squaring up for a fight. Their squeals were horrible, and we could actually hear the thuds as their hooves struck into each other. There was no way we were knowledgeable enough to break up this fight, which looked like it might end up being fatal, so we backed out of the car park and went to find a phone. It took us maybe 20 minutes to get back to the motel and call the authorities. Imagine how silly we felt when they called us back later to say that there were no zebras or anything else up there, and the zoo certainly hadn't reported any missing. It was bizarre, and I have no idea what happened or what we saw that night.

This sounds like an unlikely tale, but I believe them. Obviously there are no native wild zebras in Arizona, and as far as I know there never have been. I suspect that one of three things happened. Either this could have been the ghosts of two zebras who once lived at the zoo – perhaps when it was on a slightly different site. Or, like wallabies in England, perhaps so many escaped captivity over the years that there actually are now some zebras in the wild. The third option is this: could this have been a visitation from another dimension? Another Arizona, where there are wild zebras? After all, scientists now believe that there are many different dimensions, and many alternative universes.

The following story came from Crystal George, and so far it's the only ghost animal story that's come out of Africa.

I was brought up among game farms and was quite used to seeing big cats. They never scared me because I always knew how to act around them. There was just one, just once, that really freaked me out. I was visiting a friend's holiday complex and got there a bit earlier than she said to, so I was just hanging around until she got back from town. I went down to the water hole to see if anything was around. There were some zebras drinking, and that was about it. I sat down in the brush to watch. After a while I saw a shadow slinking through the trees. I squinted, trying to make it out. It looked like a lion. I was thinking this was totally fantastic, because I knew how long Patty's family (who owned the park) had been wanting their own lion. Over here, mad as it sounds, people who have fenced off some of the wilderness often have to buy animals to put in it. All the wildlife is actually owned by someone around here. Patty's mum and dad hadn't been able to afford a lion yet, so I was really pleased to see that obviously they had one now.

The lion, still in the shadows, seemed to be creeping up on the zebras. That put me in a difficult spot. It's an unwritten law that you don't step in and stop a lion (or any other predator) hunting. They have to live, after all, and it's up to the owners to make sure there are enough prey animals to maintain a balance. If you wanted lions, you had to be willing to sacrifice the odd zebra. I hated to see it, though. Lions are actually pretty kind the way they kill. They don't savage their prey like some big cats; they grab hold of the nose and suffocate them. But still I didn't like to see it. I looked around and no one was watching. The lion was sneaking up on the cutest baby zebra and I thought I'd just save this one. It was only a baby, after all. I knew that if I made a lot of movement the zebras would run off, so I started jumping up and down, pretty confident that the lion, who was the other side of the water hole, wouldn't even think of coming after me – I was too close to the cabins.

It worked perfectly, and the zebras ran for the hills. But the funny thing was, the lion took no notice either of them or of me. He continued his prowl as if the zebras were still there. I couldn't make it out. By now I could see he was a beautiful specimen, healthy and well-fed, so Patty's family had done well to get him. Then I could see that the lion was about to spring, but on nothing! He leapt, and vanished – all that was left was a cloud of dust. I couldn't believe my eyes. I must have blinked or something and missed him, I thought. Lions can move really fast, but still, the nearest cover had been yards away.

At that moment Patty came walking up behind me. I told her how pleased I was that she'd got a lion at last. She looked puzzled, 'What lion?' she asked, 'We won't be getting one for months yet.'

This is another fascinating story. I have to ask, though, was this a lion's ghost? Had a lion once prowled that land and come back to haunt it? Or was this a vision from the future?

I have a special admiration for birds, and I particularly have a problem with people shooting them for sport. I'm sure no one would argue that a bird in flight is one of God's greatest wonders. Man has always envied and tried to emulate their power, starting right back with the legend of Icarus. Even modern-day planes can't capture or imitate the majesty of a gull soaring acrobatically on the wind over the sea. Birds don't have to pollute the skies by burning fossil fuel to achieve their miracle, either, and yet some people seem to feel they have the right to reduce this living wonder to a spiralling mess of feathers by shooting it out of the sky in the name of sport. I hope this following story from Kevin will make some of them think again.

To tell the truth I'm a little ashamed of what I'm about to tell you. For maybe 20 years I bred birds in an aviary in the garden. I had canaries, budgies and some finches. I became quite the expert and thought I knew everything there was to know about them. They were breeding successfully, and were healthy, so I must have been doing the right thing, mustn't I? People came from all over to buy my birds and it was a successful little business. I sometimes felt a small pang when people bought one to keep indoors in a cage, but I didn't feel so bad that I didn't take their money. I did sometimes think that birds, being sociable, might not be so happy on their own, but it wasn't as if birds had souls or anything, was it?

Anyway, all my birds had been captive bred, so they knew nothing else. They didn't, couldn't, miss being free. I

always told people to be sure and let them out to fly sometimes and to seriously think about buying a companion.
But most people wanted them to learn to talk, and they
don't talk so well if they have a companion.

I had one particular bird that was my best breeder. She was
a little blue bird, and I had her for 12 years. That's a long
time for a budgie to live. I'd bred her myself and she'd
lived her entire life in a cage about six foot square.

I knew the time was coming close when I would lose her,
and she was starting to look very thin and scruffy. One day
I came home from work and saw her lying on the floor
of the aviary. I went in and picked her up. She was still
breathing and I could feel her little heart pounding away,
but I knew she was on her way out, so I just waited. It was
as if she'd held on until I came home, to say goodbye, I
thought. A couple of minutes later her heart stopped.

I opened my fingers and looked sadly at her little form,
and then something moved. A shadowy shape rose up
from the dead bird in my hand and, as it rose higher, it
formed itself into the shape of a bird. It was all grey in
colour and nearly transparent, but there was no mistaking
what it was. It fluttered to the top of the cage, hovering
when it met the wire netting. I was holding my breath,
staggered at what I was seeing. The bird turned back in
mid flight, apparently looking right at me. For a second I
thought that despite its translucent look it wasn't able to
pass through the wire, but then it did. It flew on upwards,

higher and higher until it was just a speck in the distance. I shook my head, telling myself I'd been dreaming. And then off in the distance and way up high I heard her singing. Usually only male budgies really sing, but this was unmistakably a budgie singing. It was as if she was telling me how happy she was. And then it hit me. She hadn't held on to say goodbye at all. She'd held on to teach me something. My eyes filled with tears as I thought about how her little spirit had flown free. I realized how wrong I'd been. Birds shouldn't be in cages. From that day to this I've never kept another caged bird, and I never will.

Imagine how powerful this experience must have been to get Kevin to change the habit and career of a lifetime. He would have had to have been totally convinced of its reality in order to reverse his beliefs so drastically. But who could resist the sight of a little spirit bird flying up to freedom after years of captivity? Animals, it seems, will often endure years of hardship and deprivation in order to teach one of us, a member of the so-called 'superior race', a lesson. And when they do, it's done with grace and gentleness, which in itself puts them above humans in many ways.

Chapter 9

Animals That We Eat

'Life is life – whether in a cat, or dog or man. There is no difference there between a cat or a man. The idea of difference is a human conception for man's own advantage.'

– SRI AUROBINDO

'The time will come when men such as I will look upon the murder of animals as they now look on the murder of men.'

– LEONARDO DA VINCI

I make no apology for including two powerful quotes for this chapter, because this is a subject close to my heart. Another saying is that if abattoirs had glass walls all men would be vegetarians. I don't necessarily agree with that, because there are a lot of people who would still eat animals if they saw what happens to them on the way to the plate, but hopefully what would happen is that people who wanted to eat meat would make sure the animals were treated humanely at all times. This wouldn't just be for the good of the animals, but also for the good of people's souls, not least the farmers who are forced to intensively farm to make a living, and the slaughterhouse men who have the actual blood on their hands. For we are all intertwined inextricably together, connected by our roots. We depend on the animal kingdom for so much, and they depend on us too.

All souls, whether starting from a spark in the clay or housed in a lion or a dog, are on a journey towards being finally contained in the body of a human. Not because we humans are necessarily the top link in the chain, but because only as a human can our souls experience what they need to in order to progress any further. Having learned from our animal incarnations, we're as ready as we can be to endure the trials and tribulations of being human.

Animals that are 'progressing' towards this end can't be expected to become a good example of the very being they most fear. How can they be expected to make a 'good' human if humans have instilled fear and pain into them? So we owe it to animals and to future generations of mankind to let life forms leave this world with good memories of people.

Kevan Walden sent me this story of insight into what might become of animals that are mistreated in their lifetime.

One day, as young men do, a group of us decided to take a trip to somewhere we really weren't supposed to go. Young guys have an inherent need to 'prove themselves' in some way, and in our neck of the woods this meant a trip to the old pig- and chicken-breeding factory a few miles away. There were two things that made the place appealing. One was that we weren't supposed to be there, and the second was that it had a bit of a spooky reputation, which meant we could harmlessly test each other out to see who had the strongest nerve.

This place has been closed for decades but as we discovered, there's still stuff happening up there. It was in the middle of winter and so the night got really dark really quickly, but that was part of the challenge. We parked the car some way off and made our way on foot to the fence, egging each other on as to who should go in first. Once over the fence we went into the first building, the one where the pigs used to be slaughtered. It was strange, because after all the years of the place being shut down I swear I could still smell rotten meat. Of course, each one of us was hoping something spooky was going to happen, something that would freak the other guys out while we personally remained unafraid and so would be the winner of the macho contest. But nothing seemed to be happening, and the dark empty shed got boring after a while. There was one little tap from a cupboard, but that was just a mouse or something.

Next we decided to pay the chicken sheds a visit. This was where the poor chickens spent their entire short lives, only to end up strung up and electrocuted or having their throats slit. The images in the mind's eye were pretty gruesome. Suddenly there was the crash of a door slamming somewhere in the building. Then we were a bit scared because when we looked at the doors they were rusty and hanging off the hinges, and no way should they have still operated. Then from behind us we heard the chilling sound of a chicken clucking. The cry was soft, but it was enough to make us walk away. There hadn't been any chickens in those sheds for 50 years.

As we walked away we heard the heavy, rusted doors slam behind us as if something wanted to make sure we didn't come back.

My feeling on this is that there wasn't actually a chicken manifesting in the barn. This was more a stored energy replaying itself, energized perhaps by the presence of the visitors. The slamming doors probably coincided with what used to happen in that barn. The event was reactivated because it had an audience. Would the chicken noise and doors banging have been present if there was nobody there to hear them? That's a little like the question about a tree falling in the forest – does it make a noise if there's no one there to hear it? In any case this unusual haunting shows that battery hens do feel pain and discomfort, and this lingering distress from them, powerful enough to have etched itself into the fabric of the building, should tell everyone that all animals should be treated with respect.

Veal crates – everyone knows about them, don't they? When Paula Evans sent me this creepy story I was very pleased. It's nice to know that even baby cows have a voice.

I've always loved animals, and that made it particularly hard for me to learn that there was a farm that reared veal calves near to where I lived as a child. I could hear them crying in their crates from my bedroom in the summer when the windows were open, and it broke my heart. I think I'd have become an animal activist if fate hadn't taken a hand before I was old enough. When I was 15 the farm went out of business and I was very, very pleased. The farm was sold and the buildings were turned into barns for a purely agricultural business. The cows disappeared from the land and it was ploughed and seeded. That was fine by me because it meant no animals were being mistreated. Some people think it'll be sad if we have no more meat animals, because we won't see them any more, but I always ask, 'What would the cows prefer? To live a short miserable life full of distress and then be killed, or never to live at all?'

A few months went by, and I remember the night it happened because I was just 16 and I was allowed to my first disco in the town. This was in the 1960s and parents were a lot stricter then! I was walking home from the village and I had to go past the farm. It was summer and warm and light, but the hairs on the back of my neck stood up with a chill feeling because suddenly I heard the distinct lowing of calves coming from one of the barns. I couldn't believe it, and thought, after my first shock, that the farmer had decided to rear calves after all. *Oh no! How could he?* I really couldn't bear the idea that I was going to be hearing that plaintive sound night after night again.

The distressed cries continued, and I just had to know the truth. As I scrambled through the hedge, hoping there were no dogs in the yard, the sound got louder. By the time I reached the barn the noise was deafening, so much so that I thought the calves must be being slaughtered. Maybe they were killing them in the late evening so people wouldn't know about it! I'd soon put a stop to that – if I saw what I expected, everyone would know, I'd make sure of it!

The main structure of the barn was one of those old stone buildings, but the wall I was standing by had been built more recently and was made of slats of wood with gaps between, air gaps I assumed, to dry the crops. I peered through a gap and, as my eyes focused, the noise just stopped. The silence was ringing after the noise. I blinked, because all that was in the barn was a tidy row of farm machinery. Not an animal in sight. It was bizarre, but I was very relieved. I could only think that the distress of the calves had made their energy hang around in that place.

Was this an echo, like the chickens? Just a replay of events gone by? Possibly, but even if it was, it demonstrates that the spirits of animals are sometimes so distressed by their treatment that their pain and sorrow actually seep into walls and stones, recorded for history to make man feel ashamed one day.

This next story from Madeleine Walker isn't about an abused animal – quite the reverse, in fact. Her goat was a much-loved and much-pampered member of the family. But in some cultures goats are eaten, and in most countries there are incidences of them being treated as a commodity.

Mulberry was a very unusual and special goat. When she was first born she was bullied by the rest of the herd, but soon overcame her intimidation. In her later years she was very much the matriarch of the herd. She and our son, Cameron, were born in the same year and as they grew up they had a lot in common. Cameron went through a certain amount of bullying too, because, like Mulberry he was different – suffering, as we later discovered, from Asperger's syndrome – and, like Mulberry, he grew and developed into a confident young man, able to hold his own among his peers.

As with all animals there came a time when we had to lose our lovely goat. It was going to be very difficult because she was Cameron's best friend, and I had no idea how I was going to explain her demise to him, especially as she wasn't going to die naturally; her illness was forcing us to make the decision for her.

Homoeopathic and conventional remedies helped for a while, but while I was away for a week Mulberry deteriorated drastically, so I had to talk to Cameron about having to put her down. Of course this was dreadful, but I told Cameron that she would *always* love him and that she would *always* be there for him. I said that if you truly love someone, that love never dies.

Cameron was very grown up and accepted that it had to happen, because he wanted Mulberry to be free from pain, but he was mostly concerned that she shouldn't be shot. He couldn't bear the thought that she'd be killed by a bullet, it horrified him. I was able to explain that the kennel-man from the hunt wouldn't use a gun, but a humane bolt. Cameron was OK with this, and I arranged for the kennel-man to come when Cam was at school. You can imagine my horror when the kennel-man arrived, to discover that he was indeed going to use a gun! But the man was very gentle and caring towards Mulberry, and she was ready to go, so I decided to go ahead, thinking that Cameron need never know and excusing this lie to my son with the thought that I was doing the best thing for Mulberry and for Cameron.

However, a week later when I went in to put Cameron to bed he was shaking with rage, and he shouted at me, 'You lied to me! How could you?'

I was so shocked and couldn't understand what he was talking about.

He said, 'Mulberry came and told me there was a bullet in her head!'

I was horrified that Cameron knew the truth, so I sat down and apologized. I told him that I had only kept the truth from him to protect his feelings, and that it had been so quick, and how kind the kennel-man had been with Mulberry. But I also told him that the fact that he knew the truth was proof positive that Mulberry was still with him, as I'd said she always would be. Once he understood what I was saying, this proof was so amazing that it helped to heal the pain of his loss. To this day Mulberry's spirit still visits Cameron to support him, and he knows that he has her to chat to any time he needs to.

What an amazing story. There is a lot of evidence to support the idea that animals in general are capable of helping children such as Cameron. Even profoundly autistic children are energized and attentive when brought to horses. Even the animals' smell can have an effect. I feel that in the same way as we've hardly explored our planet, 75 per cent of it being under water, we have also barely scratched the surface of the spirituality of our incredible animal life.

Chapter 10

Your Pet and Its Soul

Now that you've read all the amazing stories I chose to include in this book, I'm sure you're as convinced as I am that your pets – and all animals – do have souls. Knowing this, the next step – if you want to take it – is for you to try and communicate with these souls, from whom you can assimilate immense knowledge.

There are three levels to achieving this:

> *mental connection of energy*
>
> *soul connection of energy*
>
> *the communal soul level.*

We all connect with animals quite naturally on the first level, because we naturally transfer our emotional energy to them. Energy travels. It travels between minds and hearts and between souls. So it's easy to connect emotionally with animals, but we usually do it in the wrong way, and so fail in actually communicating.

Whatever energy you're feeling, the animal will feel it too. If the energy is stressful and unbalanced, which in humans it usually is, the animal will become stressed and unbalanced too, and useful communication will become impossible. Transferring the common human energy patterns to the animal will only make the connection unusable.

The key to being able to do this in the right way is, really, to start off by doing nothing. It's not as easy as it sounds, though. Mastering the art of being totally still, both in mind and body, is incredibly difficult. If you can manage this, however, you'll be halfway towards real communication with your pet.

You need to learn to manipulate and control your emotional energy in order to truly communicate with animals.

Animals have the ability to live fully in the moment, and they can exist one moment in fear, one moment in ecstasy, then one moment in calmness. Minute by minute, each state is quickly and easily superseded by the next, depending on the circumstances. We humans tend to hang on to emotions, good or bad, dragging our energetic state from the present to the past and then back to the future. It makes us unstable, and when we're unstable it's impossible for us to communicate effectively with anything really spiritual, be it animal or human. That's why the key is to do nothing, to think nothing and to join our animal companions in the 'now'. Thinking about nothing is very difficult, and only really and truly mastered by adepts who devote their entire lives to achieving this state. The rest of us struggle to banish thoughts of financial difficulties, relationship problems, career issues, etc. out of our minds, but it can be done with practice.

Mental Connection

Start with the easier part: keeping the physical body still and calm. Set things up well, finding a comfortable position to sit or lie in, on a comfortable chair or bed. Shut the whole world out, except for the animal you're trying to work with, by switching off phones and, if possible, disconnecting or silencing the doorbell for a bit.

Starting with the muscles of your scalp, let a warm, relaxing light travel from there down your face and into your neck, through your shoulders and on down through your body to your toes. Let yourself sink into whatever you're reclining on.

What will your animal subject be doing all this time? Entering the same state as you, automatically, because, as I said, 'energy travels'. The calmer your body becomes, the calmer your pet's body will become. For instance, you might be working with a high-energy dog. It might be pacing the room to begin with, whining even, because when you both began the exercise, your energy was brittle. As you relax your body, you'll soon discover your dog lying still and relaxed by your side.

Once you've achieved this emotional rapport, try for mental connection. Just 'reach out' with your mind to your pet. At first little pictures or symbols will stutter through from them. Keep your expectancy to basic issues, on the instinct level: sleepiness, contentedness, relaxation. If you find yourself getting frantic, garbled messages, then you haven't made the exercise work and you should start again.

Start reflecting back at your pet those same feelings; this will enhance the connection.

Soul Connection

Once you've established a strong rapport, you can move on to the next stage, the soul connection.

Seek a deeper link with your pet and start asking questions of it. *Are you happy? Are you comfortable? Are you hungry?* Simple things like that, and not too deep. You should find that you get answers without any stress. If you don't, then go back a stage. Whatever you do, don't get impatient. This isn't easy and it takes practice. Certain animal communicators do make this *look* so easy, but you have to remember they have been following a life path to get them where they are, and every life experience they've been through has been carefully engineered by spirit to 'switch on' their latent ability.

During this stage you will be able to ask your pet deeper questions – about their health, their behaviour patterns and their future needs, as well as your own – and get answers. You'll be able to ask questions about past lives you may have spent with your pet, and discover more about your, and their, reasons for being alive this time.

This is the stage that most people can achieve, with effort, diligence and patience, and it is the one that's most useful for most people. The number of questions you can ask and get answers for will depend on how advanced your pet's soul is.

When it comes to setting up a communication link with a pet that has passed over, especially with questions you may have about a new pet, one very good tip is to keep a diary. Each night, or as often as you have time, write out your daily experiences with the new pet, or the life issues in general that you need help with, or questions to your passed pet. Then close your eyes, visualize a silver thread connecting your soul to that of your spirit pet, and wait for the answers and information to come.

One way to test yourself, to know for sure that you're making progress, is to start trying out your skills on the neighbourhood dogs. We all have one: a dog that barks when you walk by, no matter how many times you've walked past him before. If you can stand quietly in the face of the dog's barking, keeping gentle eye contact and making absolutely sure the energy you're transmitting is calm and serene, the dog will stop barking. Even more amazing, if you're in an area where the dogs are like neighbourhood gossips – one barks, they all bark – you'll find that when the first dog becomes quiet, he will then transmit his energy one by one to the other dogs, until they are *all* quiet.

Once you feel this is all working well, give yourself a real test and try out your skills on wild animals. Where we live we're lucky enough to have deer visit our garden regularly, so it's easy to practise this.

Deer will normally do one of two things when confronted by a human: flee or freeze. I've done this exercise with my dog KC with me, and it really is an extraordinary feeling if you can make it work.

Our high patio overlooks the deer's favourite grazing spot in a fallow field next door. At certain times of the day you're almost certain to find a deer there. Imagine the scene: me standing up, higher than the deer with my dog KC running around me. The deer's head whips up and she sees us. She wants to run, but then I close my eyes and establish Level 1 contact with her. She stays where she is. Level 2 is reached and the deer feels no fear at all. Even sudden movements from KC don't alarm her. She isn't frozen, her head and ears are mobile and she gazes back at us placidly. When you can achieve this with a naturally wild animal – an animal who *needs* to be afraid of people in order to survive – when you manage to override this natural instinct, it's a wonderful feeling.

The Communal Soul

When – and only when – you've mastered the first two levels and are able to slip through them as easily as a knife through butter, then you can attempt to move on to the final level, the communal soul connection. This is a very powerful place to be.

This level means using nature's link with the planet and everything on it to tap into universal knowledge and energy. Animals are more closely linked to the planet than we are. If you're able to strengthen your connection to them, you'll start to access other sources of intelligence in the universe. You'll naturally start to sense the tentative threads of connection to these other sources.

By linking so deeply with your pet you'll have formed a united front which will be enough to admit you into the energy of the universe, and allow you to get answers to deeper and more essential issues about your future, your pet's future and the future of the planet and everything that lives on it

Once you've been through this stage with your pet, whatever species it may be, your relationship with each other will never be the same again.

During this stage you can also learn to link with creatures that have collective souls, such as flocks of birds, swarms of locusts, etc. – any animal or creature that has a fragment of a soul and needs the others of its group to function as a whole. By communicating with a group you can learn things you couldn't discover on your own. You can then go on to link with trees, with rivers and with the very stars themselves.

Afterword

Sometimes one person can say something to us in a way that resonates with us, and this can enable us to grasp instantly the concept they're trying to put across. For this reason I think it's useful to have several different people's perspective. With this in mind I talked to some of the other amazing animal communicators I discovered on my journey through this book, to get their 'top tips' to pass on to you. This will, I hope, encourage you on your own journey towards communicating with your pets and other animals.

Madeleine Walker operates out of Somerset in the southwest of England. I've seen her handle a horse that bit anyone else who came within reach. This horse quietly rested its head against Madeleine's chest in complete and utter trust. Its owner had tried everything conventional, with no luck, but the horse told Madeleine what its problems really were. Here are Madeleine's top tips.

Love and respect are the two most important things to remember when communicating with our amazing animal friends, and never underestimate their wisdom! It never ceases to amaze me just how aware they are about our physical and emotional issues, and how much they love to help us in making sure we're as happy and healthy as possible. So it's only right that we should be just as vigilant for them. By learning to listen to their needs and advice, we learn so much about ourselves, and how they very often 'mirror' what's going on for us in their behaviour patterns, and even take on physical symptoms for us.

So I always recommend before you start to try and hear what animals are 'saying' that you sit quietly and really connect with your heart centre. It might help to close your eyes, so that you can really concentrate and focus on your task. Feel your heart opening like a beautiful bloom and imagine sending a silver or golden line, or beam of light, to connect with the heart centre of the animal. Imagine pouring as much love as possible along that line or beam. I also ask permission to connect with the animal, with the deepest respect.

If you're just starting and want to practise, begin with something simple, like asking what might be their favourite food or friend, or a favourite place they like to be. It might be useful to have a notepad and pen to jot down whatever comes to mind as you learn to strengthen your telepathic skills. We all have these skills innate within us; it's just that we've been programmed to think that telepathic communication is something weird, and something that only certain people can do.

Working with your own animals can be a little more difficult as your emotions can get in the way, and because you 'know' them so well, you may dismiss your findings as 'just your imagination'. However, when you receive information from someone else's animal that can be verified by the owner, even though it might have appeared to be nonsense to you, you know you can begin to trust your intuition and guidance from the animals.

Always finish by thanking the animal for its help and patience. I often feel that animals are so much more in tune with our energies and nature than we are, and that *they* are *our* teachers and guides. It must be so frustrating for them when they try their hardest to alert us to some issues that need addressing, either within the family or environment, and we fail to understand what they're trying to tell us. This can result in some very challenging behaviour from them, and many animals can put their homes and sometimes their very lives at risk by doing this. We really need to become more aware of their messages and act upon them, so practise, practise, practise!

Val Heart is an animal communicator and energy healer who operates out of San Antonio, Texas. I've spoken to people who've had their dogs, cats, horses, buffalo and even their own lives turned around after Val has communicated with their animals.

Here are some of Val's top tips.

We're all born knowing how to feel and connect with others over a distance, but as we grow up our society begins to teach us other ways to communicate and, often, we forget to 'listen' through our 'heartmind'. There are a few basic principles you'll need to be aware of if you want to begin opening up your own ability to communicate with your animal friends. First is your attitude. More than any other factor, your attitude towards animals determines your receptivity to what they have to say, and that affects their willingness to communicate openly with you. If you think that animals are somehow inferior to humans, then you'll want to check that attitude at the door! Have you ever met someone who obviously felt that *you* were inferior to them? Maybe by circumstance of birth, family or money, they were from a different class or group and they were happy to let you know that? They may have spoken down to you, or treated you condescendingly in some way? If you've had that experience, then you know that it doesn't feel very good. It may have made you uncomfortable, angry or frustrated. And I'll bet you found yourself not very willing to communicate back with them – or at least, not in a very loving way! When we're with our animals, we need to remember that they think, feel emotions and make decisions for themselves based on their experiences and understanding – just like we do! Their sense of smell, sight and hearing is many times more acute than ours (usually!), so they're more aware of things that often we're clueless about. Many animal bodies are stronger than humans, and their instincts are more finely tuned. Most animals are also aware of energies, frequencies, even entities that we are largely unaware of. Knowing that, can you honestly say that they are less intelligent than we are – simply because they are disguised in animal form? Because someone can't speak our language like we do, it doesn't make them less worthy of our esteem or admiration. Respect and acknowledge animals as fellow intelligent beings who share your planet and space. Admire their spiritual qualities and abilities, and become aware of their jobs and purposes. This one thing alone can transform and deepen your whole relationship, allowing and encouraging them to connect with you. As you allow yourself to see and respect them as intelligent, responsive beings with spiritual qualities that you can admire and learn from, you'll begin to know them at a much deeper level. And they'll respond to you like you're more intelligent as well!

Now think about your relationship with your animal friends. Are there ways you may be acting condescendingly towards them? Disrespecting their viewpoint? Overriding their needs or instincts? Asking them to do something they can't, or be something (someone) they are not? Our animals want to be heard and they want to help us. They don't need us to fix them as much as they need us to listen and acknowledge who they are. What we have to do is open up, listen with respect and be present with them.

Remember that our animals are greatly affected by us, their caregivers. What we do, say, think, decide and feel can rock their world – or anchor it. The better balanced *we* are, the less stressed *they* are. So what may seem to be a problem with them may actually be an issue stemming from their family or human networks!

If you're having a problem with your animal friend, it's a good idea to check your own stress levels. If you're having trouble coping with life's many challenges, you can be sure that your animal friends are having trouble, too. Make a decision right now to get the help you need to be more balanced in your life and less stressed. Spend more quality time doing the things you love and being with the beings you really care about.

Animals try very hard to communicate with us in every way they know how. They try body language, vocal expression, demonstrations, even gazing at us very intently with a great deal of focus, almost 'willing' us to understand them. Many animals tell me how very dense they think humans are because we just don't seem to get it. And that's because we forget that the most important element in any communication is our mind-to-mind, heart-to-heart connection. At that level communication is multi-layered, almost instantaneous, direct and honest. It includes imagery, emotions, intentions, attitudes and beliefs, followed and supported by actions. Every animal (including the human animal!) was born knowing how to connect with others at this level. Try just thinking of doing an activity you know your animal enjoys. Don't actually do it or make a move towards doing it, just think about it – for instance going for a walk, playing a game or offering a favourite treat. See yourself doing it in your mind, feel what it feels like to do it, feel how much enjoyment your animal expresses when you do the activity, and if it's food related, let yourself 'smell' how it smells and 'taste' how it tastes. Then let yourself imagine your animal's response. Notice if your animal's attention is now on you, and if their energy level has changed in any way. If they didn't notice or do anything different, don't get discouraged. Just try again, this time being certain that you have their attention before you start, or find a more quiet, less distracted time to try to connect. If their attitude is different and they're paying attention to you now, then follow through with the reward of doing what you were thinking about. And know that you've just communicated with your animal telepathically! Take a little time out each and every day to listen to and respect your animal teachers. Pay attention to what they're telling you. If they're 'out of balance' or acting up in harmful or destructive ways, then notice where in your own life you may be out of balance or incongruent within yourself. If they're offering their unique viewpoint, sharing love or joy or simply being themselves, then flow with them with gratitude and honesty.

Lynn McKenzie is based in the beautiful and mystical town of Sedona, in Arizona, a place I love, so she was an obvious choice for this section of the book. I have known Lynn to radically change the relationship people have with all kinds of living animals, but her most poignant work, to me, is where she has brought through messages from pets that have passed over.

Here are some of her top tips.

To me, tapping in to the souls of our beloved animal companions and gleaning their wondrous wisdom is an expansive gift that offers us such depth, and pure delight. I believe that for each of us it's a birthright and a task that we may all master, given the proper conditions and desires. A strong intention is a must, along with trust, and perhaps even a leap of faith. I like to describe our communion with the animals as 'making the heart connection', as it really is a language of the heart and is often very different from the spoken word. It may come to us in the form of feelings, impressions, pictures, symbols, sounds, tastes, smells or what I call 'knowings'. It may also come in everyday words that you hear by 'listening on the inside'. These words may sound like your own voice, or that of another. At the beginning of the classes I teach, I always ask participants to let me know if they've already had a communication with an animal companion, and I almost always find that most have, so chances are you have too!

To help you ramp up your own skills, here are a few tips:

1. It's important to quiet your mind; this can be done in a number of ways. My personal favourite is spending quiet time in nature.

2. Positively declare your intention, as if you're shouting it out to the universe.

3. Imagine or pretend that you have already mastered this skill.

4. Visualize a trust dial, like a dial on a radio, and reach out and turn it up to full volume.

5. Open your heart as wide as can be and visualize the pure pink energy of it flowing out and connecting with the heart of your animal companion.

6. Begin your communion by asking a few questions.

7. Look for the fleeting information that comes to you like lightning in the first moments. These are always the pearls.

8. Be aware that you may have to quiet that negative voice in your head that tries to tell you or remind you that you *can't* do this.

9. If you are feeling blocked, visualize the energy block as a cloud of coloured light, then see it dissolving or melting away.

10. If communication isn't coming easily, ask that it come to you over the next day, week or month, to take the pressure off (this has really helped my students).

11. Most importantly, enjoy, and prepare for information that will change your life and catapult you along your spiritual path to places never imagined.

12. Express your gratitude for all that you've received.

This process is also perfect for connecting with the souls of animals on the other side. This is a huge focus of my work, and suffice it to say that once our animal companions have transitioned, the guidance and teachings they have for us often increase.

Staying connected with the souls of our animal companions on the other side not only helps to ease or eliminate the pain of their loss, but can be very healing in so many other ways. I believe animals partner with us, in life, to help us grow spiritually, evolve and to help us manifest our own unique divine mission. And this role does not end with the ending of the physical; in fact, this is when it intensifies, so please be sure to try these steps with your animal companions on the other side, and be open to the wonderful wisdom they have to impart.

There is definitely a movement afoot whereby the animals are teaming up with us to advance us along our spiritual paths, and thus raise our consciousness, and I say, 'Why not go along for the ride?'

Resources and Useful Information

Animal Communicators

Madeleine Walker:
www.anexchangeoflove.com.
Madeleine's book, *An Exchange of Love,* was published in October 2008 by O Books.

Holly Davis:
www.hollydavis.co.uk

Val Heart:
http://www.valheart.com/

Charlene Boyd:
http://www.talk-to-animals.com/index.htm

Animal Intuitive

Lynn McKenzie: www.AnimalEnergy.com

Artists

June-Elleni Laine, psychic artist:
http://www.psychicartworks.com/

Jacqui Grogan, visionary artist:
http://www.edenspirit.co.uk

Jade's spiritual art:
http://www.sharnajamescreations.co.uk/

Other

The Barefoot Doctor:
http://www.barefootdoctorglobal.com

About the Author

Since the age of two, Jenny has enjoyed a spiritual connection with animals that's grown to full communication with them over the years. Based in beautiful Somerset, in the UK, Jenny lives with her husband and soulmate of 40 years, Tony, and her reincarnated dog, KC. Their one-acre garden is mostly a wildlife habitat, and people from the area often bring injured wild animals for Jenny to rehabilitate. Jenny has also hand-reared everything from lambs and kittens through to ducklings.

There's a famous scene in one of her TV shows where she has a barn owl sitting on her shoulder and a bat squirming around inside her top, while she continues with a live broadcast. Another scene that demonstrates her connection with all animals was when she was introduced to a pen of semi-wild foxes and they gathered close around her. One fox even scented on Jenny's hair to welcome her to the pack.

Jenny is an author, TV and radio presenter/guest, international columnist and spiritual consultant. Her own current life was turned around by a vision from one of her own past lives. Jenny has appeared on many TV shows and hundreds of radio shows, including those in the UK, USA, Australia, New Zealand, Iceland, Tasmania, The Caribbean, South Africa and Spain.

> 'If for just one second you can throw off the blindness
> of material wealth, and see the truly magical wonder of your
> entire being, including your connection with the planet, then you
> will no longer suffer from the debilitating modern-day malady of
> amnesia of the soul. For one shining moment you would see clearly
> for the first time.'
>
> – JENNY SMEDLEY

www.jennysmedley.com

Notes

Notes

Notes

Notes

Notes

Notes

Notes

Notes

Notes

Notes

Notes

Hay House Titles of Related Interest

The Amazing Power of Animals, by Gordon Smith

The Animal Healer, by Elizabeth Whiter

Animals and the Afterlife, by Kim Sheridan

Ask Your Guides, by Sonia Choquette

Power Animals, by Steven D. Farmer

The Unbelievable Truth, by Gordon Smith

We hope you enjoyed this Hay House book.
If you would like to receive a free catalogue featuring additional
Hay House books and products, or if you would like information
about the Hay Foundation, please contact:

Hay House UK Ltd
292B Kensal Rd • London W10 5BE
Tel: (44) 20 8962 1230; Fax: (44) 20 8962 1239
www.hayhouse.co.uk

***

Published and distributed in the United States of America by:
Hay House, Inc. • PO Box 5100 • Carlsbad, CA 92018-5100
Tel.: (1) 760 431 7695 or (1) 800 654 5126;
Fax: (1) 760 431 6948 or (1) 800 650 5115
www.hayhouse.com

Published and distributed in Australia by:
Hay House Australia Ltd • 18/36 Ralph St • Alexandria NSW 2015
Tel.: (61) 2 9669 4299; Fax: (61) 2 9669 4144
www.hayhouse.com.au

Published and distributed in the Republic of South Africa by:
Hay House SA (Pty) Ltd • PO Box 990 • Witkoppen 2068
Tel./Fax: (27) 11 467 8904 • www.hayhouse.co.za

Published and distributed in India by:
Hay House Publishers India • Muskaan Complex • Plot No.3
B-2 • Vasant Kunj • New Delhi – 110 070.
Tel.: (91) 11 41761620; Fax: (91) 11 41761630.
www.hayhouse.co.in

Distributed in Canada by:
Raincoast • 9050 Shaughnessy St • Vancouver, BC V6P 6E5
Tel.: (1) 604 323 7100; Fax: (1) 604 323 2600

***

Sign up via the Hay House UK website to receive the Hay House
online newsletter and stay informed about what's going on with
your favourite authors. You'll receive bimonthly announcements
about discounts and offers, special events, product highlights,
free excerpts, giveaways, and more!
www.hayhouse.co.uk